The Governor's Solution

The Governor's Solution

How Alaska's Oil Dividend Could Work in Iraq and Other Oil-Rich Countries

TODD MOSS

Editor

CENTER FOR GLOBAL DEVELOPMENT
Washington, D.C.

The Governor's Solution: How Alaska's Oil Dividend and Iraq's Last Window: An Oil-to-Cash Reader may be ordered from:
Brookings Institution Press
c/o HFS, P.O. Box 50370, Baltimore, MD 21211-4370
Tel.: 800/537-5487; 410/516-6956; Fax: 410/516-6998;
Internet: www.brookings.edu

Library of Congress Cataloging in Publication data are available
ISBN 978-1-933286-70-9 (pbk. : alk. paper)

1 2 3 4 5 6 7 8 9

Printed on acid-free paper

Typeset in Sabon and Strayhorn

Composition by R. Lynn Rivenbark
Macon, Georgia

Printed by R. R. Donnelley
Harrisonburg, Virginia

Contents

Preface

Recent discoveries of oil and mineral deposits across Africa and other developing regions have brought increased urgency to the question of how to ensure that natural resource wealth benefits citizens instead of being wasted or stolen by corrupt elites. Each new discovery is greeted with a chorus of warnings about the risks of "the resource curse" but few concrete suggestions for how to avoid it. The Center for Global Development's Oil-to-Cash initiative explores one innovative option: distributing resource rents to citizens to build a powerful constituency that serves as a check on the government's management of the resource revenues.

This idea, which Arvind Subramanian and I proposed for Iraq in 2004, is in part inspired by a similar scheme in Alaska that distributes a share of income from a state sovereign wealth fund to each resident. The dividend's apparent success in tying the hands of politicians in spending Alaska's oil wealth suggests that other oil producers could adopt a similar scheme to ensure that oil revenues serve the interest of the wider citizenry and not just those in power. This book shares Governor Jay Hammond's remarkable first-hand account of the creation of Alaska's Permanent Fund dividend alongside recent work exploring the feasibility of an Alaskan-type solution to the oil curse in other settings, particularly Iraq. In tying historical narrative to concrete policy proposals, it serves as a companion volume to the forthcoming *Oil-to-Cash:*

Fighting the Resource Curse through Cash Transfers, where Todd Moss and others lay out the proposal in more detail.

We thank Larry Smith and the Hammond family for reaching out to us with the governor's manuscript, which spurred the idea for this book, as well as the Revenue Watch Institute, which first commissioned the chapter by Scott Goldsmith. This work is part of the Center's ongoing research on natural resource management in developing countries, which benefits from the financial support of the United Kingdom's Department for International Development and our other supporters.

Nancy Birdsall
Center for Global Development

1

What's Alaska Got to Do with . . . Iraq?

Todd J. Moss

This book came about because of an email I received out of the blue in September 2011 from Larry Smith, an Alaska-based journalist asking if I might be interested in reading an unfinished manuscript by Jay Hammond, who served as governor of Alaska from 1974 to 1982. Of course, I knew of Hammond, famously nicknamed the Bush Rat Governor, as the political force behind the Alaska Permanent Fund dividend. Through this program, every Alaskan resident receives an annual check, which is a share of profits from the state's oil-revenue-fed sovereign wealth fund. The 2011 dividend for each resident was $1,174.

Although half of the fund's profits are distributed to residents, it has also been a boon for state finances. In fact, Alaska now earns more from its offshore fund than it does from direct oil income.

But more important than the money itself, the dividend—or more precisely, the expectation of a regular dividend in the future—has led to a huge amount of public attention and thus provided a powerful constraint on Alaska's politicians. That was Jay Hammond's vision.

Back to that email—Smith explained that Hammond had been working on a book telling the inside story of the dividend and laying out his ideas for how lessons from Alaska—including his own mistakes—might be useful to other countries struggling to find ways of holding public officials accountable for their management of oil revenues. In particular, Hammond believed that his experience was relevant for Iraq, a country

1

2   Todd J. Moss

on the forefront of policymakers' minds during the period Hammond was writing, 2003–05. The governor died in August 2005, however, before completing his work. Smith explained that the Hammond family later asked him and a few others to lightly edit and publish the manuscript. In 2011 copies were printed and sent to every library in the state of Alaska—an important contribution to recording state history.

Smith asked if the Center for Global Development might be interested in distributing the Hammond text to a wider audience. CGD's Oil-to-Cash initiative is a multiyear effort exploring how one policy option may address the root mechanism of the resource curse in poor countries: using cash transfers to hand the money directly to citizens and thereby protect the social contract between the government and its people. Under this proposal, a government would transfer some or all of the revenue from natural resource extraction to citizens in universal, transparent, and regular payments. The state would treat these payments as normal income and tax it accordingly—thus forcing the state to collect taxes on the cash transfer along with any other income and providing additional pressure for public accountability and more responsible resource management. The Oil-to-Cash initiative draws from experiences in places such as Mexico, Brazil, Mongolia, and elsewhere, where large-scale cash transfer programs have been initiated, some linked to resource income. But the closest real-world example of Oil-to-Cash is, of course, Alaska. The idea owes much to Hammond's innovation and inspiration. His manuscript was thus the firsthand account of an idea that CGD is now championing.

Nevertheless, as with any unsolicited email, I was initially skeptical of Smith's offer. I did not know him and, as a rule, CGD does not normally accept or publish unsolicited manuscripts. But I was intrigued enough to agree to read the manuscript and hoped, frankly, that I might skim through it and glean a few insights into Hammond's political strategy that might be applicable today. Instead, from the very first page, I couldn't put it down.

Hammond's story walks the reader through his early experimentation—and failure—with citizen-shareholder schemes, starting in small Alaskan fishing villages through to his (mostly accidental) road to the governorship, and his ultimate success in implementing one of the world's great experiments in democratic governance. What struck me initially was the straightforward, and frequently self-deprecating, writing style. Who expects a history of a revenue management scheme to be so engaging, let alone laugh-out-loud funny?

While Hammond's raw writing style is fun to read, the real reason an economic policy think tank in Washington, D.C., is publishing this book is the power of Jay Hammond's ideas. His explanations of why he believed that giving citizens a direct stake in the state's natural wealth would help to create a virtuous cycle of accountability are particularly revealing—and prescient. As a Republican deeply concerned with equity and citizen stewardship, his ideas transcend partisan politics. At the same time, his story explains the deeply political context and the tactics he deployed to overcome entrenched interests. These provide important insights today, because any politicians trying to implement a similar scheme will face hurdles and bargaining trade-offs not dissimilar to those tackled by Hammond thirty years ago.

Perhaps most important, Hammond is reflective and brutally honest about his mistakes. He bluntly admits that his failure to veto the repeal of the state income tax was, in retrospect, wrong. Although the tax repeal was part of the deal that paved the way for approval of the Alaska Permanent Fund, he believed that without a state income tax, he allowed the state to cut "the cord that attaches the public's purse to the fingers of the politicians."

Herein lies a critical lesson for those of us who believe that a version of an oil dividend might be a useful idea for some of the new oil-producing economies: cash transfers must be accompanied by broad and transparent taxation. Indeed, for many poor countries that strike oil, building a tax base is precisely the point. Without taxation, citizens have little incentive and even less capacity to hold the government accountable for public spending. Taxation is the basis for accountability. Which brings us from Juneau to Baghdad.

Iraq is a country that relies on oil for nearly 90 percent of government revenue, and less than 4 percent comes from regular taxation. It is also a society deeply torn by regional and other divisions. In other words, it is a prime candidate for an Alaska-type dividend to help unify the nation and build a social contract. Hammond too came to this conclusion, and the final section of his chapter provides his thoughts on how Iraq might learn from Alaska's experience.

To complement Hammond's personal account, the remainder of this volume brings together recent work by scholars on Alaska and Iraq, tackling the same issues around cash transfers from different perspectives. Scott Goldsmith of the University of Alaska at Anchorage, a leading expert on the Permanent Fund, provides a retrospective analysis of Alaska's experience (courtesy of the Revenue Watch Institute) in chapter 3. Chapter 4 is an article by Nancy Birdsall and Arvind Subramanian that appeared in *Foreign Affairs* in 2004 and originally proposed that an oil dividend be implemented in Iraq (reprinted here courtesy of the Council on Foreign Relations). Of course, despite some support at the time within the Iraqi and American policy communities, this option was not chosen. However, chapter 5, by longtime Middle East journalist Johnny West, under commission by CGD, examines the possibility that the idea could be revived soon. West argues that an expected increase in production provides a new opportunity for Iraq to try this idea in coming years. Crucially, West also identifies growing political support within Iraq for a national dividend, including some unexpected champions.

Together, the writings here provide a compelling case that much still can be learned from Alaska's experience and its visionary former governor. It is a powerful reminder that new ideas combined with determined individuals can make a tremendous difference—even with issues as seemingly intractable as the oil curse. Combating the corrosive effects of easy money on governance in both rich and poor countries is a problem that still requires much more innovation as well as inspired political leaders. I hope that this book makes a small contribution in that direction—and that readers also share the serendipitous enjoyment this book provided me.

2

Diapering the Devil: How Alaska Helped Staunch Befouling by Mismanaged Oil Wealth: *A Lesson for Other Oil Rich Nations*

JAY HAMMOND

Preface

"I call petroleum the devil's excrement. It brings trouble. . . . Look at this *locura*—waste, corruption, consumption, our public services falling apart. And debt, debt we shall have for years."

So warned Juan Pablo Pérez Alfonso, a Venezuelan founder of OPEC. A September 24, 2004, article in the British magazine *The Economist* elaborates further on Pérez Alfonso:

> During the heady oil boom of the mid-1970s . . . he was seen as an alarmist. . . . In fact, he was astonishingly prescient. Oil producers vastly expanded domestic spending, mostly on gold-plated infrastructure projects that set inflation roaring and left mountains of debt. Worse, this did little for the poor. Venezuela had earned over $600 billion in oil revenues since the mid-1970s but the real income per person of Pérez Alfonso's compatriots fell by 15% in the decade after he expressed his disgust. The picture is similar in many OPEC countries. So bloated were their budgets that when oil prices fell to around

Editor's note: This chapter has kept as much as possible Hammond's original text even though it was an unfinished manuscript.

Acknowledgments from Larry Smith, coordinator

The Hammond Family: Bella Gardiner Hammond, Jay's wife, who keeps the home fires burning and who asked her granddaughter, Lauren Stanford, to send me the author's last draft. Lauren went on to help with editing and thoughts for an epilogue. Her mother, Heidi Hammond, supplied insights and photographs for the Alaska edition. David McRae, a nephew, whom Jay Hammond called "my surrogate son," is Jay's successor as the family pilot, mechanic, and man of all basic bush work. He takes the lead in sending the philosophic message of Jay Hammond to the intended audiences. *Rock-Ribbed Independent Friends:* Clem Tillion, close friend and ally who calls Jay "my big brother," and Lowell Thomas Jr., Hammond's first lieutenant governor, who provided advice, encouragement, and donations to defray printing costs.   *Historians and Providers:* Jack Roderick, Stephen Haycox, and Michael Hawfield, who provided fact-checks and/or early reviews. The Alaska State Library provided 158 mailing labels and the packaging and postage to send a copy of the first edition to every library in Alaska. The Kachemak Resource Institute donated the books. The Homer Alaska Public Library sent out copies.   *Proofreading and Editing Crew:* Lauren Stanford, Pamela Brodie, Jackie Pels, and Mary Maly. In addition, Mary did the layout and text and cover design for the book distributed in Alaska.   *Sine Qua Non:* My partner, Pam Brodie, worked on all phases. By her I was out-punctuated, out-spelled, out-thought, and out-grammared—but not out-enamored. At that I prevailed.

$10 a barrel in 1998, a number of countries—including Saudi Arabia, the kingpin of oil—were pushed to the brink of bankruptcy.

But it was long before Alaska struck oil that events prompted actions that ultimately served to at least modify the adverse effects cited above. In essence, Alaska managed to avoid much of the befouling of Pérez Alfonso's "devil's excrement" by actions that served to at least halfway pin on a "diaper."

Oil Wealth Windfalls: Blessing or Bane?

It all started with fish. Perhaps the greatest inducement for Alaskan support of statehood in 1959 was the prospect of abolishing salmon traps. Alaskan fishermen had long resented the virtual monopoly enjoyed by

Seattle-based fish barons. Not only did they sop up the bulk of the salmon harvest with devastatingly effective fish traps located at the mouths of prime spawning rivers, but in Alaska's Bristol Bay, home waters for the world's largest wild sockeye salmon run, the canneries blatantly favored nonresident fishermen over Alaskans when it came to assigning the company's fleet of wooden drift gill-netting sailboats.

Prior to 1952, allegedly for conservation purposes, Bristol Bay gill-netters were not allowed to use power, and while the vast fleet of sailboats embarking at sunrise on the morning tide may have been picturesque, mortality rates were high, while income to Alaskans was pitifully low.

In our quest for statehood, we Alaskans piously attempted to make the case for fish trap abolition on the basis of conservation. It was a phony argument. Actually, fish traps provided far better segregation of salmon stocks and management of harvest to allow for adequate escapement to individual river systems than did a drift gill-net fleet. A wish to get a bigger piece of the action, not concern for the resource, was our major motivation.

This hypocrisy, along with other questionable assertions by most advocates and the utter rejection of any consideration of Commonwealth status, prompted me to oppose statehood. When asked my reason for doing so I rudely questioned our ability to finance and administer statehood. Not even the scent of oil had yet seeped into our nostrils. Instead, Alaska's major sources of income: fishing, mining, and trapping, all were in steep decline. Moreover, I imprudently pronounced, "With our tiny population of under 100,000, virtually any idiot who aspired to public office was likely to achieve it." Subsequently, there have been those who assert I proved that upon frequent occasion.

While the gush of oil wealth in the late 1970s provided the potential for financing state government, the jury is still out as to whether we have the ability to administer state government prudently. Perhaps the best inducement, indeed obligation to do so, lies in Article 8, Section 8, of Alaska's constitution, which states: "The legislature shall provide for the utilization, development, and conservation of all natural resources belonging to the state, including land and waters, for the maximum benefit of its people." While this does not actually say the people rather than government own those resources, as many contend, it amounts to virtually the same thing.

This mandate first prompted me to attempt to assure that *all* Alaskans received a discernible share of those benefits. That battle, I lament, continues here in Alaska despite growing worldwide awareness of the potential for other resource rich nations to follow Alaska's example, and thereby largely avoid the common past practice of selectively benefiting the favored few at the expense of the many.

Bristol Bay's Blighted Bonanza

Though I had little aspiration for political office at statehood in 1959, much to my bewilderment and no little dismay, I found myself elected to the Alaska House of Representatives as an independent. I had not campaigned at all, but told the local school teachers urging me to run that I would *consider* doing so only if they were willing to collect the number of prospective voter signatures required to place my name on the ballot as an independent. They came back the next day with the petition for me to submit. My "consideration" in their minds had translated into "commitment" and, though I had made none, I knew they would feel I had broken my promise should I fail to run. So, with no fear of winning, I ran and, to my great surprise, won.

It was with much reluctance that I left the good life I had in bush Alaska as a commercial fisherman, pilot, and guide, where I not only could call my own shots but also build my own targets. Moving my family to Juneau, adhering to the legislative schedule, and, perhaps worst of all, enduring daily strangulation with that abomination of the western world—the necktie—did little to enchant me. Thus, it came as no small surprise that I found the legislative process intriguing.

Most intriguing were efforts to comply with that aforementioned constitutional mandate that I thought was being largely ignored. A select few, mostly from outside Alaska, were reaping the benefits of our resource development—too often at the expense of the many. Fisheries were a prime example, though they, unlike mining or timber, at least yielded a modest raw fish tax to the state. Not surprisingly, the prime issue addressed by the first Alaska legislature was that of fish traps, which provided fortunes for their nonresident owners and returned little benefit to Alaskans.

When Nick Bez, a powerful and persuasive spokesman for the Seattle-based salmon industry, testified before the legislature urging us to phase out rather than instantly abolish all fish traps, he made an excellent case. I complimented him but advised he was wasting his time. "Sorry Nick, but even if we were persuaded by your arguments, you'd simply have to go through this drill all over again before the brand new legislature which would replace us."

Accordingly, one of our first actions was to outlaw fish traps. However, their abolition did little to improve the lot of many Alaskans. Nonresidents remained favored by Seattle processors in assignment of company boats, and few Alaskans could afford to compete with the ever-increasing costs of larger, faster, and better-equipped company-financed power boats.

While in the legislature, I proposed several measures designed to give Alaskan fishermen a better competitive edge. Virtually all were struck down as unconstitutional, and rightly so. Either they violated the U.S. Constitution's Interstate Commerce Clause or they abused the "privileges and immunities" of nonresidents. Obviously a different approach was required.

That approach was found in the taxation power vested in local governments. In 1962 the Bristol Bay villages of Naknek, South Naknek, and King Salmon—total population about 2,000—banded together to form Bristol Bay Borough, the first of its kind in Alaska (a local government entity similar to a county). Inducement to obtain local control was not the only carrot provided by the legislature. At my behest, it also doubled the amount of state-collected raw fish taxes returned to a borough and enacted a statute that allowed a municipality to impose a "use tax."

Prior to becoming a borough, despite the extraction ("use") of literally billions of dollars of salmon wealth from our waters, our communities were little more than rural slums. We had no high schools, sewer or water systems, health care facilities, fire, police, or ambulance services. Garbage was dumped over the riverbank in hopes it would flush out with the ice during high spring tides. Such conditions prevailed when I took over as borough manager in 1965. While I would like folks to think altruism was my major motivation, the prime factor, of course, was simply money—or rather, lack of it. A study presented to me by my borough assemblyman, Martin Severson, indicated that a whopping 97 percent of the fishing payday made within the boundary of the Bristol Bay Borough went elsewhere: 65 percent to nonresidents and 32 percent to those living in Alaska but outside the borough. Local residents got but a paltry 3 percent!

The solution seemed simple: Impose a use tax of, say, 3 percent to be paid by all fishermen on their catch. For every $3 paid in taxes by locals, we would glean $97 from nonresidents. To offset the impact on local fishermen already paying high property taxes, I proposed putting tax money into a conservatively managed investment account, then each year issuing residents one new share of dividend-earning stock. I called the concept "Bristol Bay, Inc." It fell flat on its face. The ordinance required to impose the tax went down to crashing defeat at the polls. All people could hear was the word "tax."

So adverse are most Alaskans to taxes that even should one be devised which made them money most would oppose it. Naively, I thought this was simply due to ignorance. Hence, in hopes of providing enlightenment, I took to the stump, wrote newsletters, and spoke to interest groups, carefully explaining what seemed a wondrous potential for not only remedying the borough's pitiful lack of services, but also bolstering the finances of every resident, whether they fished or not.

To my dismay and consternation a second vote on the use tax ordinance went down by an even bigger margin.

Reluctantly, I abandoned the Bristol Bay, Inc., stock-sharing concept and presented two new ordinances in what I hoped would be an offer the public couldn't refuse. Ordinance "A" would impose the 3 percent use tax. Only if ordinance "A" were to pass would Ordinance "B" kick in, which would then abolish all local residential property taxes.

Most locals checked their records and, finding themselves far better off with both the use tax and elimination of residential property taxes, approved both ordinances. The results exceeded my wildest imagination. Almost overnight the Bristol Bay Borough was transformed from that virtually destitute rural slum into what *Fortune* magazine termed "The richest municipality in the nation on a per capita basis." Unfortunately, however, instead of providing all residents with equitably distributed discernible dividends from which they could pay for services desired, almost all our newfound wealth went into inequitably dispersed government programs.

My salary as part-time borough manager had been but $6,000 a year. My total budget was $35,000. From this, I hired a secretary for $12,000, paid legal fees, and employed a part-time bookkeeper. Our largest expense was installation of a chain-link fence to keep bears from strewing garbage from the riverbank onto the road. But a few years later, after I had left my borough job and returned to the legislature, the borough manager's salary was $81,000. Twenty-one full-time employees were hired and the annual budget exceeded $4 million. However, the borough had also built a high school, acquired fire and police protection, and provided a sewer system, health care, ambulance services, docking facilities, and perhaps the finest state-of-the-art garbage disposal system to be found in Alaska.

These may have been worthy accomplishments, but, nonetheless, they were programs that provided individuals with inequitably distributed selective benefits. Moreover, the residential property tax relief local citizens had been promised was denied when the legislature passed a bill limiting residential property tax relief to but $10,000. This was designed to strike a blow against the exceedingly wealthy and powerful North Slope Borough, which some feared would boost its property taxes excessively on oil facilities, while exempting local residents' homes.

That legislation provided the Bristol Bay Borough Assembly with grounds to deny the total residential property tax exemption I had promised and, in effect, made a liar out of me. In an attempt to remedy this some years later, I proposed that the assembly at least give fishermen a credit against their property taxes equal to that which they paid in fish use taxes. Assembly members smiled indulgently, allowing that such was an interesting proposal, but did nothing to prevent fishermen being double-barreled with both use and property taxes. To their credit they did, however, heed one suggestion. The conservatively managed investment portfolio envisioned under Bristol Bay, Inc., was established. Ultimately this grew to $12 million.

Believing other fishing communities could prosper if they adopted a similar use tax, I appeared before the Alaska Municipal League, outlined what we had experienced in Bristol Bay Borough, and suggested the league might wish to follow suit. Curiously, it was years before any other municipalities did. Today, however, virtually all municipalities encompassing fisheries have done so. Meanwhile, fishing communities had lost hundreds of millions of dollars in prospective revenues, which they could have gleaned almost painlessly, largely from those who lived elsewhere and profited from doing business within the municipality.

Difficulties I've experienced in attempting to sell programs, which seemingly would be ardently embraced by beneficiaries, suggest I am a lousy salesman. Evidence of this frailty next became evident when I attempted to peddle the Bristol Bay, Inc., concept to Alaska Natives.

Again—No Sale

With passage of the Alaska Native Claim Settlement Act (ANCSA) in 1971, Alaska's aboriginal peoples were accorded 44 million acres of land and $900 million by the U.S. Congress. This measure was the culmination of years of effort by Native leaders to secure reparations for past abuses and broken promises. Actually, however, passage was finally facilitated by the need to acquire permission from prospective Native landholders to cross lands over which the proposed Trans-Alaska Pipeline would be built.

After passage of the Settlement Act, the debate then commenced as to what the Native Alaskans wished to do with their money and land. Some of my Native constituents from the village of Nondalton, some twenty-five miles away, visited me at our Lake Clark homestead to seek my counsel. My first response was: "Don't ask me, a *gusuk* (nonnative), to try to tell you how to handle your money and lands. That's for you to decide."

They were not about to let me off the hook. "Look, you're our representative and are not at all shy in suggesting how the Bristol Bay Borough handles its wealth. Surely you have some ideas. What are they?"

I responded, "It seems to me you have two prime options. You can split your assets and form a multitude of mini-bureaucracies with the attendant administrative and legal costs; or you can follow the concept I proposed for the Bristol Bay Borough: create a conservatively managed investment account and spin off equal dividends to every Alaska Native. Such an account should be managed by professionals under counsel supplied from an elected advisory board of Natives representing every group in Alaska. That way you can lift yourselves up by the bootstraps rather than depend on government handouts."

With a population explosion accompanying a decline in fishing, trapping, and ability to live off the land, many Native leaders decried what they perceived as growing dependence on government programs, which could make drones of some of the most self-sufficient of the Earth's peoples. The area's primitive housing, lack of gainful employment, sewer or water systems, health care, adequate schooling, fire-fighting equipment, and police protection all served, by contrast, to point out the comparative affluence of Appalachia in the southern United States.

Why not, instead, make stockholders of all Alaska Natives and thereby provide them with the means, along with the responsibility, to use it for their collective best interests? After all, if they have the capability of meeting some of their needs from their own pocket and the responsibility to do so, it would seem freedom of choice and self-determination could do much to retain self-respect, while meeting what the people themselves felt to be their primary needs—far better than "Great White Father" paternalism.

I so stated the same in an article appearing in the *Tundra Times*, a now defunct publication that played a key role in uniting Alaska Natives in pursuit of justice. While a few Native leaders were intrigued with the investment account and equitable stock-sharing concept, opponents mounted persuasive arguments. Whether these were primarily prompted by deep concern for Alaska's indigenous people or self-interest is debatable. Certainly there were those who salivated over prospects of obtaining high-paying jobs, pocketing lucrative legal fees, or promoting pet projects.

There also were, perhaps, those who feared the enormous financial and political clout Natives would have were they to consolidate to form a monolithic entity, permitting them to move and shake in those realms as never before. They argued persuasively that each corporation should be able to spend its share of the wealth as it saw fit: "You don't want others from elsewhere telling you what to do with it," was the refrain. By accepting that counsel, the enormous political and financial power potential was splintered, though still remained a considerable force.

Ultimately, rather than creating a single investment portfolio managed by a board of directors comprised of Native leaders from throughout the state, which would spin off equal dividends to every Alaska Native, the majority bought the argument they should not permit others to determine how their share of the wealth would be used. As a result, instead of the equitable stock-sharing concept proposed in Bristol Bay, Inc., some fourteen regional and over 200 village corporations were formed, much to the delight of a multitude of salivating attorneys, along with those who obtained lucrative corporate jobs.

While a few corporations have prospered handsomely and a number of exceptionally competent Native business and political leaders have emerged, in some cases poor investments were made in fly-by-night schemes that would not have passed muster had they been scrutinized by a money-managing control board composed of non-locals. Lack of experience in handling large sums of money, nepotism, and village politics sometimes prompted imprudent, low- (and even no-) interest loans and investments that served to place some corporations on the brink of bankruptcy. And though virtually all corporations have paid stockholders dividends, there is an enormous disparity. Some have distributed annual dividends as high as $50,000 to every shareholder, while others provided less than $500.

By contrast, had the equitable Bristol Bay, Inc., concept been adopted and the pooled settlement monies experienced growth, comparable to Alaska's subsequent investment of a portion of its oil wealth in what is now known as the Alaska Permanent Fund, every Alaska Native would probably be receiving thousands of dollars annually in dividends. Ability to invest in sound economic development would not in the least have been hampered. Instead, many of the unsound investments that have been made no doubt would have been avoided had others, able to overlook local politics, screened them from elsewhere. Receipt of dividends—the size of which was dependent on the prudence of such investments—would assure such screening.

Had the land claims money earned on par with that of the Alaska Permanent Fund, I am told the initial dividend would have been about $1,154 per shareholder for that year. Not many years later, a prominent Native legislator studying the issue asserted the dividend would then have been about $5,400. If so, by now it might well be five figures. Dividends of that magnitude not only would have taken many off welfare, but would have provided communities with enough financial resources to have assumed municipal status and, with the accompanying taxing authority, provided services that they were willing to pay for and that villagers believed were in their best interests. Instead, many villages became increasingly dependent on government-funded entitlements.

Nothing gives folks a greater feeling of accomplishment and worth than self-determination, sense of ownership, and personal responsibility. When obligated to fund and maintain power plants, schools, community centers, local roads, and airfields from their own pockets, people are likely to count coins more carefully and maintain standards in which they can take pride. When government provides those programs gratis with few strings attached, inequity, duplication, and inefficiency too often become a matter of course. The latter approach has not only shackled many villages to dependence on both state and federal largesse, but has encumbered Alaska with government service costs per capita far in excess of any other state.

Artificial Respiration

Elsewhere, when ore bodies deplete, natural catastrophes strike, or bread baskets become dust bowls, often people depart leaving ghost towns in their wake. Not so in Alaska. We simply do not let villages die.

Of the over 200 villages in Alaska, few have viable economies. Private sector jobs are exceedingly scarce. As a consequence, unemployment in Alaska is perennially the nation's highest. By contrast to many Alaskan villages, Appalachia is affluent. With their burgeoning growth, Alaskan communities find it increasingly difficult to subsist off adjacent lands or waters. Accordingly, many villages are heavily reliant on government spending.

In hope of addressing some village problems, some time ago the state legislature attempted to persuade villages to band together and form organized boroughs (similar to counties) under the threat that if they did not do so, the state would perform all the functions of the borough assembly, including imposition of property taxes. Though the law has been on the books for more than forty years, not once have legislators elected to act in that capacity. To do so not only would be highly unpopular, but also with the scant property values found in many villages, taxes accrued would probably not cover cost of collection. As a consequence, the state or federal government picks up the entire tab for most services, including education.

To assure that the more affluent rural areas with a sufficient tax base participate in helping fund government services, just as do folks in urban centers, a statewide property tax to help finance schools had been proposed. However, one size hardly fits all. Levying a property tax sufficient to fund schools in all villages could cripple the poor ones. Yet I believed a tax system could be devised that would provide equity, while recognizing some communities needed more help than others. I therefore proposed that we first determine what the total statewide property values were per capita. Then should, say, a 3 percent statewide property tax be imposed for those communities in which they generated *less* than what they would if local per capita property values were the same as those statewide, the state would fund the difference. Conversely, should that 3 percent tax generate more than that overage, the overage would go to the state. That way, all would be taxed the same, but affluent municipalities, such as the North Slope Borough with high oil property values, would have to assume more of their local government service costs than would those virtually destitute.

That proposal also fell flat on its face and perhaps rightly so. Costs of statewide assessment and administration might have sopped up even more state money. Unfortunately, inequitable taxation has continued to help create what some term an urban/rural divide. Many in Alaska's urban areas resent what they feel are inordinately high local property taxes required to fund their schools, while the state provides substantially greater support for those many rural communities unwilling to tax themselves. Yet who can blame the latter so long as the state will pick up the tab? This disparity, coupled with federal legislation that provides that on federally owned lands "rural residents" are granted highest, and sometimes exclusive, priority in the harvest of fish and game, has further frayed the state's social fabric.

In another effort to reduce crippling costs of attempting to provide services to hundreds of economically unviable communities—not connected by roads and lacking adequate housing, schooling, and basic services—I once proposed we determine which regional centers had the most viable economic potential and focus on providing them with top-notch schools and other services. For example, in the Bristol Bay region the village of Dillingham had a population of about 6,000 and the Bristol Bay Borough, which at that time encompassed a now closed Air Force base, a population of about 2,000. None of the other twenty-some villages in the region had a population of more than 300 and some less than 100. First-rate educational, transportation, social, medical, sewer and water, police, and fire suppression services could be provided to these centers, thereby encouraging those who aspired to these emoluments to move thereto. Others who wished to retain the "village lifestyle" cherished by many rural folk would not be obliged to move, but would not be provided housing and service subsidies of a comparable nature.

Once again my proposal fell flat. Instead, at enormous per capita cost, we have attempted to provide similar services to each and every community regardless of size or potential. The result has in many instances been both inadequate and inequitable.

For instance, in my one-time hometown, Naknek, within the Bristol Bay Borough, the state and municipality fund K–12 education, maintain airfields and roads, provide police and fire protection, ambulance services, and garbage collection. One mile across the river, in South Naknek, and then thirty miles south of the village of Egegik, both with populations of less than 200, we struggle to provide the same. Another thirty miles south we do likewise for Pilot Point, population of about 100. Forty miles further down the Alaska Peninsula these service costs are again duplicated in Port Heiden, population less than 200. And so on throughout over 200 small villages in rural Alaska.

Further compounding costs to the state, and reducing the inclination of villagers to move, was institution of what is known as the Power Equalization program. This provided that in communities where costs of electrical power exceeded a certain amount, the state would pick up a portion of the overage. This did little to promote efficiency or conservation. Instead, it was but another attempt to make it more likely people would remain in their home villages rather than migrate to a more economically viable area.

The cost of providing these services in village after village with little, or perhaps no, economic base for existence is astronomical. The argument for continuance of such seemingly wasteful practices is that if the villages were allowed to die, many villagers would be compelled to move to urban areas and go on welfare at perhaps even greater expense to the state. Unfortunately, there is likely some truth to that argument. Meanwhile millions upon millions of dollars are poured into rural villages unable to financially fend for themselves.

Partially in an effort to provide villagers with both the capability and responsibility for meeting some of the needs they deemed most crucial, when I was elected governor in 1974 I proposed a program patterned after my failed attempt to create Bristol Bay, Inc., while mayor of the Bristol Bay Borough. I called it "Alaska, Inc."

Alaska's First Dividend Program

Shortly after becoming governor in 1974, I learned that Alaska charged one-half the national average severance tax on our natural gas. The main reason for this was to provide lower cost gas to Anchorage consumers. However, most of our gas was being shipped to Japan. While I did not so much oppose giving Alaskans a subsidy, I had little enthusiasm for providing a similar subsidy to the Japanese. Moreover, most Alaskans, though "owning" the gas, were not beneficiaries of the subsidy and therefore were being denied that "maximum benefit" obligated by our constitution. This prompted introduction of legislation to double Alaska's gas severance tax to match the national average.

However, Anchorage legislators were not about to pass such a cost increase on to their constituents, even though that increase reportedly amounted to but $19 per year for the average gas-consuming family. To no one's surprise, the bill was quickly buried. Clearly, an offer they couldn't refuse seemed in order. To accomplish this, we introduced two bills: one doubled the severance tax and the other, contingent upon passage of the first, granted everyone in the state a "dividend" in the form of a $150 credit against their state income tax. Both passed and millions of new dollars flowed into state coffers. Two million dollars went out in tax credits; the remainder increased the state's general fund. The only ones unhappy were the Japanese.

Subsequently, however, I found almost no one remembered the tax credit. At that point I decided that if another dividend program were established, I wanted to put a check in *everyone's* hand, rather than simply a credit for those making sufficient income to pay a state income tax. I thought that by so doing people would better recognize and appreciate the dividend concept and demand the state maximize returns from its resource wealth.

I believed the best, perhaps the *only*, way to meet our constitutional mandate to manage our natural resources for the maximum benefit of all the people was to grant each citizen an ownership share in Alaska's resource wealth to be used as they, not the government, felt was for their maximum benefit. To accomplish this objective, I proposed that 50 percent of all mineral lease, bonus, royalty, and severance taxes be deposited into a conservatively managed investment account. Each year one-half of the account's earnings would be dispersed among Alaskan residents, each of whom would receive, annually, one share of dividend-earning stock. The other half of the earnings could be used for essential government services.

While I believed we should have put all our oil wealth into such an investment fund and lived off its earnings, it was obvious the legislature would never forgo the opportunity to spend a sizeable portion of that oil wealth. Only by permitting them to do so could I possibly hope to get any significant amount into that investment account.

My rationale for creating such an investment account and making shareholders of Alaskans was manyfold:

1. I wanted to encourage contributions into the investment account and to protect against its invasion by politicians by creating a militant ring of dividend recipients who would resist any such usage if it affected their dividends.

2. I wanted to transform oil wells pumping oil for a finite period into money wells pumping money for infinity. It was apparent that unless we did so, politicians would spend every windfall to satisfy insatiable short-term needs and demands, only to find themselves in a world-of-hurt when oil wealth declined. Such had been the experience of virtually every oil-rich state and nation. Not only Pérez Alfonso's Venezuela had been defiled by "the devil's excrement."

3. To put it crudely, I wanted to pit collective greed against selective greed. In the past, those who knew how to play the game were able to secure subsidies for their pet projects, many times at the collective expense of all other Alaskans. One example of this was a program granting loans not based on need at an interest rate far less than what that money could have earned in an investment account such as proposed in Alaska, Inc. In one year alone, more money had been lost to the state through subsidized loans not based on *need* than was paid out that year in dividends, and those loans went to but 6 percent of the people.

4. I wanted to remove a number of Alaskans from welfare. (The legislature subsequently frustrated this effort by exempting dividends from consideration as income when determining one's eligibility for welfare.)

5. By issuing shares of dividend-earning stock annually and allowing Alaskans to accumulate them over time, I hoped to eliminate the magnetic attraction for others from elsewhere who might otherwise be

inclined to flock to Alaska in order to receive dividends. Few would do so for the mere $50 dividend per share we initially set arbitrarily, but many might if everyone received a few thousand.

6. I wanted to install a sense of ownership in all Alaskans that would incline them to support healthy resource development and resist unhealthy versions. To determine whether such development was healthy, I cited four criteria that should be met: A. Was it environmentally sound? B. Did the majority of Alaskans want it? C. Could it pay its own way? D. Did it meet our constitution's mandate that it provide maximum benefits to the people? All the people?

7. I wanted to eliminate controversial state expenditures for such things as abortions. Many sorely resent use of their state dollars for this purpose. Let individuals aspiring to an abortion pay for it instead, from their dividends. Keep the state out of it.

To promote these concepts, fashioned after my failed Bristol Bay, Inc., proposal, I created "The Alaska Public Forum." My intent was to travel about the state holding public meetings in an attempt to glean support for a constitutionally enshrined Alaska, Inc. This, of course, required not only support from two-thirds of the legislature to place the proposal on the ballot, but also voter approval. Despite my efforts, response from most Alaskans was either derision or a massive yawn. Accordingly, I simply proposed a statute to accomplish my objectives. Legislative support, to say the least, was underwhelming. Fortunately, however, there were some legislators who felt more prudent handling of any resource wealth windfalls was in order.

This attitude came in the wake of a $900 million windfall we received in 1970 from leases issued in Prudhoe Bay. Though a handful of us then in the legislature agreed with then Governor Keith Miller that we should invest at least half of this bounty and spend only its earnings, the majority of legislators quickly sopped it all up in pet projects. Chief among these was to disperse money to municipalities in revenue sharing, which helped to lower taxes but gave little evidence to voters of anything concrete occurring or being constructed. As a result, many felt the windfall had been "blown."

Reflecting on voter displeasure, several legislators swore that if another windfall were to blow our way we would not make the same mistake. Nonetheless, such caution virtually blew out the window when the next windfall blew in. To their credit, however, a sufficient number of legislators were successful in passing legislation creating what they termed "The Alaska Permanent Fund." This statute at least created a semblance of Alaska, Inc., but fell far short of what I had hoped for. The 50 percent contribution of oil lease bonuses, royalties, and severance taxes that I had proposed was cut to 25 percent, and severance taxes, which constitute roughly half of our oil wealth income, were eliminated and instead funneled into the general fund. Moreover, no stock-sharing dividend program was included in the legislature's statute.

Though, by now, I had been working on trying to sell the investment account stockholder concept for fifteen years and finally a first step toward that objective had been taken—I vetoed the measure in one of the most painful actions I felt forced to take. I did so because I feared that absent stockholder concern by all Alaskans over how the fund was utilized, we would simply create a semipermanent fund, allowing continuance of past practices that saw special interests with the most political clout invading the fund while the general public was largely short changed. Therefore, I insisted that the legislature place on the ballot a proposed constitutional amendment that, if passed by voters, would not only enshrine the fund in the constitution, but also require a public vote before any of the fund's corpus could be spent. While I wished to include a dividend program in that amendment, it was evident the legislature would never pass the measure with such a provision.

In the next general election, voters approved the amendment and the fund was established. Next came the chore of trying to secure a dividend program. Once more, I confronted not only apathy but also strong resistance in the legislature. Nonetheless, I proposed legislation that provided that one share of dividend-earning stock would be issued each year to all Alaskans over eighteen years of age. My hope was to create an annuity account to be dispersed when children reached the age of eighteen. I also wanted eligibility to receive shares to be contingent on providing evidence one had voted in the previous general election. I thought nothing could do more to boost our pathetic average 40 percent voter turnout or provide greater capability for our youth to either go on to college or into the workplace with the several thousand dollar cushion they'd receive when coming of age. Some contended the voting contingency would perhaps boost voter turnout to over 100 percent by those attempting to vote more than once. (I later learned that it would be impermissible to base eligibility for receiving dividends based on evidence one had voted. The

Alaska Supreme Court had struck down such an attempt when the North Slope Borough had offered to pay every voter $5. However, I'm told that it would be permissible to hinge eligibility for dividends upon having *registered* to vote.)

Initially, most legislators were vehemently opposed to the dividend program. Delegations came to my office on more than one occasion assuring me there was no interest in passing such legislation. My response was to advise them that unless they at least permitted the dividend legislation to come to the floor for a vote, they would be called back into special session the day they adjourned, and, moreover, those who voted to keep the bill in committee could expect all their goodies to be stripped from the budget. My good friend Clem Tillion, who was at the time state senate president, delivered this message with gusto. In doing so, Clem earned the title of my "strong right arm and swift left foot." Largely as a consequence of Clem's efforts, the bill emerged from committee and passed by a substantial margin.

Believing "old-timers" should receive one share of dividend earning stock for each year they had lived here after statehood in 1959 when they, in essence, by constitutional mandate, became owners of our resource wealth—just as new-timers would in the future—I had provided that "shares" would be issued retrospectively back to statehood some twenty-one years before. Each share's dividend was arbitrarily set at $50. (Later the size of dividends would be determined by dividing the number of shares issued into approximately one-half the previous five-year average earnings of the Alaska Permanent Fund.) I agreed that the other half of those earnings not dispersed in dividends could be used for essential government services. Thus, those who had been here since statehood would initially receive twenty-one dividends yielding shares totaling $1,150.

This feature prompted two newcomers to the state, Ron and Penny Zobel, to challenge the constitutionality of the program. They charged it improperly discriminated between Alaskans on the basis of durational residency. Superior Court Judge Ralph Moody agreed. However, the Alaska Supreme Court overruled Moody in what Chief Justice Jay Rabinowitz said was a close call. The case then went before the U.S. Supreme Court, which ruled against the state. Chief Justice Rabinowitz informed me that had we issued "shares" *prospectively* commencing in 1980, we would have been on solid ground, but that the U.S. Supreme Court deemed issuing "shares" retrospectively impermissible.

This conclusion seemed completely irrational to me. After all, old-timers here before statehood would have received only twenty-one "shares" in their twenty-first year of residency, whereas newcomers in their twenty-first year would have received 210 shares: one the first year, two the second, three the third, and so on. Accordingly, if anything, under our original program old-timers were discriminated against.

While I admire those who, through courage of conviction, espouse politically unpopular remedies for what they view as injustice, the nobility of the Zobels' cause would have gained much luster if they, as federal employees receiving 25 percent salary adjustments tax free because of Alaska's high cost of living, had been equally concerned that all Alaskans were not granted such consideration. Nonetheless, their efforts probably accorded the Permanent Fund even greater protection by expanding benefits to a far greater number of dividend recipients, including children.

With the U.S. Supreme Court's negative ruling, it was back to the drawing board. The legislature next passed a measure that granted every qualified Alaskan a dividend of $1,000. This amount was deemed to approximate three years' worth of dividends from one-half of the past five-year average of the fund's earnings. The other half has been available for legislative appropriation but to date none of it has been so spent. Public fear that any such use will reduce their dividends has made legislators extremely gun shy. Those who have received annual dividends since their inception have received more than $21,000 in total—a family of four, more than $80,000.

When first considering the idea of dividends, I had explored the possibility of providing all Alaskans with basic health insurance or credits against, say, their heating or power costs. However, once again this would fail the equity test since many already had health insurance coverage under government or private sector plans, and the additional bureaucracy required to administer such programs would be counterproductive. In the end, it was concluded that the most equitable distribution of benefits was the cash dividend to be used as the recipient, not the government, thought best.

One of the major objections some have had to dividends is the potential magnetic attraction that would lure many "freeloaders" to flock up here to receive dividends. This would have been avoided under the original program in which one share of dividend-earning stock would be issued for each year one resided here. When the court struck that down, that magnetic attraction became a real concern.

While I did not necessarily recommend it, I suggested a legal means by which that attraction could be eliminated in but a year or two. First, we could announce that all who wished to qualify for dividend "A" must do so during the ensuing twelve months. Then the door for qualifying for dividend "A" would close. Perhaps when the Permanent Fund had grown by, say, 10 percent, we would then issue dividend "B," the amount of which would be determined by dividing that 10 percent by the new total number of Alaskans eligible. Those who qualified for dividend "A" would also qualify for dividend "B." As dividend "A" recipients died off or left the state, their shares would be added to the dividend "B" pool and so forth.

While this certainly would reduce the magnetic attraction of the current program, it would, of course, to a degree serve to divide Alaskans and possibly splinter support for maintaining the integrity of the Permanent Fund.

Uneconomic Development

In 1980 the legislature abolished Alaska's income tax, which I, at the time, asserted was the most stupid thing we could do. Reduce or suspend it but don't take it off the books completely, for it will prove almost impossible to resurrect, no matter how desperately needed. When asked what are some of the things I most lament not having done during my term in public office, I'd have to place my failure to veto income tax repeal high on that list.

Some felt I was contending Alaskans were stupid by endorsing income tax repeal—not at all. Even brilliant people can do stupid things. Just ask Bill Clinton. However, unlike Clinton, Alaskans were thinking with their wallets instead of their heads.

While income tax repeal certainly benefited a number of Alaskans financially in the short term, with it the state embarked on the road to what I term "uneconomic development." This is development that does not generate sufficient new revenues for the state to offset the cost of providing services to the attendant population increase or for managing, enforcing, or enhancing resources being exploited. The late revered State Senator John Butrovich pled with us not to repeal the income tax, recalling that almost all those old-time legislators who had nerve enough to support its institution were defeated during the next election. Despite Senator Butrovich's pleas and my arguments against tax repeal, the legislature gleefully repealed it. As I recall, only two legislators voted against it.

Why did I not veto that repeal? Simply because I didn't have nerve enough to confront accusations that I had broken a commitment to permit it to become law if our bill suspending the tax was struck down by the court. Unable to believe that would happen, when a reporter asked, "If the court strikes down the tax suspension bill, would you permit it to become law?" I responded, "Since there is a repeal referendum on the ballot supported by almost every Alaskan, I might just as well, since I'm sure the legislature would love to jam a veto override down my gullet, if the public did not first impeach me."

To my dismay, the court struck down our bill. That same reporter again confronted me saying, "You said you'd let the repeal become law if they struck the suspension bill down. Do you intend to keep that commitment?"

While I actually had made no such commitment, it would have always been believed by some that I had broken my word had I vetoed it. Accordingly, despite my misgivings, I did not. For this lack of courage I apologize to all Alaskans for placing a false charge impugning my integrity ahead of their best long-term interests. I should have subordinated my concerns to theirs and vetoed the bill in a last-ditch effort to avoid creating a condition that not only encouraged legislators to spend as if there were no tomorrow, but also ultimately placed the Permanent Fund in harm's way. Though a veto would not have stopped income tax repeal, it might have caused many more Alaskans to recognize the folly of abolishment.

While arguing against tax repeal I had stated,

> Many Alaskans believe we are spending beyond our means. I agree. To correct that, you either reduce spending or increase your means. By repealing the income tax we did precisely the opposite. We reduced our means and severed the major constraint on runaway spending: the cord that attaches the public's purse to the fingers of politicians. No longer requiring them to tweak that cord each time they wish to increase spending, it sailed into the stratosphere. In the process we also

promoted "uneconomic development" by failing to extract enough new revenue to offset costs imposed on the state by new development and its attendant population increases. Instead we shoveled in "one-time-only" oil dollars to pay for them.

This action, of course, is what created the fiscal gap—a gap that would have been little more than a fissure had the income tax been suspended like a Damoclean sword over the legislature, threatening to decapitate them if they permitted spending to spin out of control.

> This is why I feel so passionately that we create of our Permanent Fund a true 'People's Portfolio,' which could assure a bright future for our children's children by virtually guaranteeing we invest much of our oil wealth in their future well-being rather than throwing it in the maw of the fiscal gap.

Having stated all the above, there remained another, perhaps the primary, reason for not exercising my veto power. The Alaska Permanent Fund program had not yet been ironed out and I feared many legislators—preferring to spend those dividend dollars as they, rather than individual Alaskans, saw fit—would torpedo the entire program.

Our failure to meet recurrent expenditures with recurrent income seems lost upon many Alaskans. The prime factor obscuring this dangerous situation is our ability to balance the books from monies that have gone into an account called the Constitutional Budget Reserve (CBR). This account is comprised of funds received from settlements made on behalf of the state from several suits lodged against oil companies, most during the seventies, but some only settled years later. Into that fund have gone several billion dollars.

The CBR was established by constitutional amendment as a repository for "one-time-only" oil litigation settlement dollars. According to law, any funds extracted from the account are loans to be repaid by the legislature. In essence it too is a "Permanent Fund." However, it is the best example we have as to just how impermanent such funds are when not protected by dividend recipients who would never tolerate failure to repay loans from the fund if it hit them directly in the pocket book, as would extractions from the Alaska Permanent Fund. To date not one cent has been repaid to the CBR. Instead, it has steadily dwindled from several billion dollars to but only a couple. Each year for the past several, legislators have dipped into the CBR to span an annual fiscal gap of several hundred million dollars. Our ability to do this has obscured from Alaskans the fact that we face a fiscal crisis unless we mend our ways and get back on track, paying for recurrent government expenses with recurrent income, not ephemeral, one-time-only oil dollars.

It is easy to understand why most Alaskans seem unaware of the folly of continuing past imprudent practices. After all, most of us came from states that were forced to pay for government with recurrent income. The vast reservoirs of finite oil wealth that could be ladled from obscured the fact that we were foolishly funding government from unsustainable sources.

Compounding the problem is the fact that most Alaskans fail to recognize that there are really two state economies. The private sector economy does wondrously well when our population expands; more goods and services are sold, and those selling them prosper. However, while the private sector economy flourishes when population increases, the public sector economy (that is, government) would be far better off financially if our population were to decline. This is the case because the cost of providing government services vastly exceeds the amount of new revenue gleaned from taxes to offset the cost of these services. Instead, we pay for those services with finite oil dollars that are the same in magnitude whether we have 600,000 people up here or 6 million.

The picture is further distorted by the fact that there are two public service economies: local government and state. While the local public sector economy may prosper by development that adds to the local tax base, the major costs of government services, such as education, are borne by the state, and the impact of local growth on the state public sector economy may, and often does, impose a loss on the rest of the state.

Until these economies are brought into balance, all growth and development proposals should take into consideration the collective impact on all citizens of the state, not simply local populations.

A Proper Role for the Permanent Fund

Without a state income, sales, or property tax, the only sustainable funding source Alaska has, currently, is the Permanent Fund. Certainly it should play a key role in our financial prospectus. Given my preference, I would have imposed on all our natural resources sufficient taxes to contribute enough money to the Permanent Fund to cover costs for mitigating environmental concerns, management, enforcement, or enhancement, plus an equitably distributed public benefit as mandated by our constitution. To date, only oil does so. Timber, minerals, and fisheries have contributed not one cent to the Permanent Fund. Instead, oil indirectly subsidizes all other development.

One environmentalist friend not long ago criticized me for emphasizing economic over environmental concerns when discussing prospective development projects. He asked, "Why do you no longer emphasize quality of life and vision for the future? Instead, you seem to focus primarily on economics."

Unfortunately, some are prone to forget that there is more than one dimension to the environment. It encompasses not only the physical environs but also the economic and social. None should be ignored when evaluating some prospective economic development project. By overemphasizing the former over the latter, environmentalists are too often contemptuously written off as "tree huggers," "preservationists," or "greenies."

In Alaska, to some developmental "extremists," the label "environmentalist" ranks just under "child molester," and it is contemptuously appended to any who oppose their pet projects. When asked if I am an environmentalist my response is, "Of course. Isn't everyone?" However, my concerns are not confined to just the physical environs; there are also social, economic, and spiritual dimensions to the environment. Too many of us tend to focus on but one or two dimensions and ignore the others.

Too many emphasize the adverse physical and social impact of some proposed development project they deem destructive over the long-term overall economic impact. In my view, they would be wiser to place greater emphasis on economics. Many projects that strike horror in their hearts are salivated over by special interests that stand to profit handsomely. Only if it can be shown that such a project costs the majority of Alaskans more than it profits them economically will folks—who couldn't care less about the "dickey birds"—sit up and take notice. Under Alaska's current tax policies, many proposed mega projects that would perhaps provide enormous benefits to a select few would no doubt cost the rest of Alaskans. They would not generate enough new revenue to offset the costs of state involvement in providing infrastructure, maintenance, permitting, enforcement, and tax-free state services for the attendant population increases that accompany such projects, as new folks and their families flood up here seeking jobs.

As I mentioned before, although Alaska's constitution mandates we manage all our resources for the maximum benefit of the people (and in my view that means *all* the people), from the very beginning that mandate has been largely ignored. For example, early on Alaska had imposed a 1 percent severance tax on oil, a modest raw fish tax, a tiny stumpage fee on timber, and a nickel-a-ton tax on coal, the rationale for these taxes being that we could adjust our tax structure later after companies started to do business up here. I believed this precisely backward. Instead we should have started out with, say, a 99 percent severance tax and worked our way slowly down until we started to get vibrations. At that point, we would have a far better idea of what the appropriate level of taxation might be to encourage development that met the constitutional mandate to maximize benefits. Once having determined that level, we should have stuck with it. Instead, since we really had no idea how many eggs we could snatch from these golden geese without endangering the species, we changed our taxation policies repeatedly and, at this writing, are contemplating doing so once again. How much better it would have been for both the state and industry to establish a stable tax that met the constitutional mandate yet encouraged development. At the level the state felt met that mandate, industry could either pursue development or leave the resource in the ground, on the stump, or in the water.

Initially, I had proposed that a severance tax of at least 12 percent be levied on all nonrenewable resources and one of 6 percent on "renewables" such as timber and fish. These would all go into the Permanent Fund and thereby give every Alaskan a sense of resource ownership, with the attendant support for resource development that could meet those four criteria I felt crucial to assure healthy resource development:

Is it environmentally sound?

Do most Alaskans want it?

Can it pay its own way and not require state subsidies?

Does it provide maximum benefit to the people?

I failed, however, to get my severance tax proposal passed, and Alaskans really have no idea whether we are maximizing our benefits from any form of resource development. The Permanent Fund provides about the only lens through which the public could and would view more realistically the true costs versus expense of development, but unfortunately, only in the case of oil.

One example of a popular project that clearly failed to meet those criteria was a petrochemical plant proposed for the Kenai Peninsula that would create scores of high-paying new jobs. Since the mantra of many politicians is "Jobs! Jobs! Jobs!" they fail to ask the question "At what cost?" In this particular case those costs were substantial. The only way the plant would be economically feasible was if the state would agree to sell our royalty oil at a discounted rate, which translated into a $240,000-per-year subsidy for each job created. When, as governor, I turned the proposal down, some viewed it as but another example of "Hammond's anti-growth and development policies." If stifling growth was truly my objective, I failed miserably. Growth during my administration, fueled by excessive spending of nonrecurrent oil wealth, was unprecedented.

Clearly, in the minds of most Alaskans, oil development does a pretty good job of meeting those criteria. That is why most endorse oil development in the Arctic National Wildlife Refuge (ANWR). Certainly oil has contributed monumentally to Alaska's economy, even if it does not fully meet that constitutional requirement for *maximization* of benefits to all Alaskans.

Hooked on Handouts?

Are we Alaskans hooked on handouts? You bet! But dividends are like a barbless fly compared to gaffing done by income tax repeal. Consider: Though $80 billion in oil wealth has been spent for unequally dispersed state service "dividends" worth over $7,000 per capita, for which we pay almost nothing, not one cent has gone out in PFDs! Only some earnings from investments of our other $30+ billion in the fund go for these equitably distributed dividends. Addiction to free services burgeoned with tax repeal. That action created far greater "something for nothing" dependence than dividends.

Again, our constitution mandates that Alaska "manage its resources for maximum benefit of its people." Asked what's the maximum benefit they've received from oil, no doubt most would say dividends. Certainly, no program better meets that mandate. Couple that with the fact that dividends yield the biggest bang for the buck in stimulating our economy, and that any reduction in dividends would have exactly the same effect as a "head tax" paid by only and all Alaskans in the same amount, whether prince or pauper, one would think politicians would use dividends last rather than first as budget gap fill. Yet increasingly dividends are dubbed "The worst thing we ever did" by House Speaker Pete Kott. Former House Speaker Brian Porter said, "The difference between us is we'd use dividends first. You'd use them last." And an ex-governor (who shall remain anonymous) terms them a "cancer" on Alaskans' image as rugged individuals.

If dividends are a "cancer," that cancer—by contrast to tax repeal—is but a penny-sized skin lesion. To subject it to radical surgery before treating the multibillion dollar fiscal gap, a tumor bloating our bellies, seems asinine. Though PFDs may have caused that skin lesion, tax repeal proved far more carcinogenic by conditioning us to believe we are entitled to those huge, free, inequitably distributed service "dividends." Had we, instead, *suspended* the income tax pending its need, spending would have been greatly curtailed and there would likely be no fiscal gap. After all, the best therapy for containing malignant government growth is a diet forcing politicians to spend no more than that for which they are willing to tax. In that regard, I once suggested that, depending on location of brain, every politician have branded on either their brow or their buttocks the pledge: "I will not spend more than that for which I am willing to tax."

Before slicing dividends to cure that skin lesion, let's first treat that belly tumor with surgical budget cuts and, if necessary, the "radiation" of user fees and less regressive taxes. Let's leave dividends in the people's pockets so they can both better afford and, to a degree, elect whether or not to pay coming user fees and taxes.

At every forum, discussion, seminar, and committee meeting I have attended during which means of bridging our fiscal gap was discussed, there was much less enthusiasm for reimposing a broad-based tax than reducing dividends. At the end of each of these I posed this question: "Will someone here please tell me when it ever makes more sense to cut dividends and use those dollars to span the fiscal gap, thereby imposing a head tax on every Alaskan while exempting transient pipeline workers, construction stiffs, and commercial fishermen, rather than using tax dollars?" The answer, of course, is "Never!" Yet far more effort has been expended by the legislature to do the former, while the latter has been largely ignored.

That is not to say that the dividend program is without defect. It was badly bent when the original program was struck down. That would have treated the Permanent Fund as the people's investment portfolio by granting all a share of dividend-earning stock for each year they "invested" in Alaska. When the Court ruled against us, I was so distraught I considered vetoing the substitute bill creating the current program. However, since I thought dividends would still best protect the fund from erosion by government spending, I approved it.

Most agree that without dividend recipients fending off invasion, the fund would long ago have been spent. Accordingly, dividends impose an effective spending limit. Unfortunately, however, this spending constraint was largely offset by tax repeal that eliminated that major curb mentioned earlier: limiting politicians to spending only that for which they are willing to tax. Accordingly, should we need dividend dollars for government programs, lawmakers should have to retrieve them through user fees or targeted taxes. Instead, Speaker Pete Kott said he would convert the Permanent Fund from a sacred cow to a cash cow to balance the budget. Problem is, who gets to fondle the udders—the people or the politicians? It makes little sense to pay out ever-increasing dividends if we have in place no means of recouping whatever is necessary to fund essential government programs.

Before high oil prices bailed them out, legislators, fearful of voter outrage for either imposing taxes or using Permanent Fund earnings for government, were compelled to cut popular programs. While howls of anguish from those affected had not yet become deafening, they increased as scalpels sliced ever deeper into state programs. Before those scalpels became meat axes, I had hoped that voters would ease off on the rack on which the legislative body was being stretched, lest it burst asunder and bloody us all. Ratcheting down on one end of that rack were those who would permit no use of Permanent Fund earnings, save for dividends and inflation proofing. At the other end were those who have conditioned politicians to view even the suggestion of taxes as akin to self-immolation.

I make no apology for being among the first group because it always makes more sense to use a tax dollar for government spending than it does a dividend dollar since the latter costs every Alaskan, and only

Alaskans, a dollar. About twenty cents of each tax dollar could be raised from outsiders, and the rest from those of us who can best afford it. Our problem is not with those who would stand at one end of that rack, but those who would stand at both ends. We cannot have it both ways. If we do not want politicians to touch our prospective dividends, we must back off on our opposition to taxes, or vice versa.

Meanwhile, we should not so much blame legislators for painful budget cuts. We have put them in such a bind on that rack, they see no political alternative but to try to stretch fewer and fewer available dollars over the straining body politic. Only when the pain inflicted exceeds that of either new taxes or invasion of Permanent Fund earnings will tension ease off. Unless we soon provide some wiggle room, in an attempt to slice their bindings, the scalpel they wave will not only excise fat but slice deeply into the meat and muscle of government.

Disbursing Permanent Fund Earnings

Virtually every governor since my term has promised to require a public vote before any fund earnings could be spent for other than dividends or inflation proofing the fund. Some had to be coerced into doing so. My successor, in 1982, Governor Bill Sheffield, had originally opposed the dividend and came within one vote of abolishing it before he got religion and concluded that action would be political suicide and that dividends played a key role in Alaska's economy, annually trickling *up* from the grass roots hundreds of millions of dollars. Economists assert the dividend program provides the greatest bang for the buck of any state expenditure.

Governor Steve Cowper, who succeeded Sheffield, tried at the end of his term in 1990 for a constitutional amendment to put some Permanent Fund earnings into an education endowment, but he failed to get the necessary two-thirds vote in the state senate to get it on the ballot.

In 1990, former Secretary of the Interior and former Governor Walter Hickel called a press conference to announce he had decided to run for governor on the Alaska Independence Party ticket, primarily because President George H. W. Bush's White House chief of staff, John Sununu, had called him, urging him not to run for governor against Republican primary winner, Arliss Sturgelewski. Affronted by this, Hickel pronounced, "I had not planned on running, but no one tells me what to do, so I'm filing under the Independence Party ticket." At that time, I had great apprehension regarding the future of the Permanent Fund under Hickel as governor. Though these were later happily reconciled, his comment prompted me to hold a press conference of my own.

During that particular campaign three prime issues dominated. Each night there would be two opposing talking heads on television being queried as to their positions on those issues: re-criminalization of marijuana, abortion, and who would qualify for the subsistence use of fish and game resources when inadequate supplies would not permit all Alaskans to do so. At my press conference I got reporters' attention when I stated:

> I've called this press conference to announce my intentions regarding entering the gubernatorial race as a write-in candidate. Some have suggested I do so. But I'm like Wally Hickel. I don't like to be told what to do, so I'm not going to do it!
>
> Now that we've disposed of one inconsequential matter, I'd like to address three others. During this campaign the prime focus has been on three issues legislators are unlikely to address at all: certainly they won't touch abortion with a twenty-foot pole; recriminalization of marijuana is on the ballot as a public referendum; and subsistence will likely be resolved by the courts, if at all. How individual legislators stand on these issues will in all probability make not the slightest difference. On the other hand, only one candidate, Tony Knowles, has mentioned how legislators intend to enhance and protect the Permanent Fund.

While several reporters interpreted this as an endorsement of Knowles, it was not. I simply wanted to get all candidates on record regarding their intentions regarding the Permanent Fund. A few days later, there appeared in the paper a full-page ad by candidate Hickel announcing that he would veto any appropriations of the Permanent Fund for other than inflation proofing or dividends.

When Hickel later became governor, he adhered to that promise. Knowles, who succeeded Hickel in 1994, did so as well and in 1999 insisted that a fiscal plan passed by the legislature, including use of fund money that otherwise could be used for dividends, be placed on the ballot. It was defeated by a whopping 83 percent of the voters, largely because no lid had been placed on the amount of dividend dollars that could be so spent.

During the pre-election debate on the matter, I debated the governor and appeared a dozen or so times on radio, television, and various public forums, urging voters to disapprove the proposal unless there was an acceptable lid placed on the amount of earnings that could be used for other than dividends. Though I, and I am sure most other Alaskans, got sick of hearing me repeat, ad nauseam, arguments on this matter, I was happy when they prevailed. Voters remained so concerned that any such use would reduce their prospective dividends, most legislators for years have been reluctant to spend even that portion of Permanent Fund earnings not required for dividends.

Past attempts to use earnings failed to pass muster largely because they either would have reduced dividends beneath what they would be under the current method of establishing dividend size, or they created unpredictability. One approach proposed would continue to take the past five-year average fund earnings and divide that in half; one-half to be dispersed in dividends while the reminder could be spent for government services. However, fluctuations in the stock market make such payouts imprecise and unpredictable.

Largely in order to reduce such unpredictability, the Permanent Fund Board has recommended a different approach for determining annual dividend size. They proposed the Permanent Fund be treated as an annuity as are many investment funds. Traditionally these provide that 5 percent of the fund's market value (POMV) can be dispersed annually on the assumption that it will annually earn an average of 8 percent and the 3 percent differential will offset inflation.

Recently rejected, however, was an effort to transform the Permanent Fund into such an annuity in order to make payouts more predictable. A proposal to disperse annually 5 percent of their market value (half as dividends and half for state services) failed to pass the legislature since opponents quickly discerned that dividends would in a few years be hundreds of dollars less under the 50/50 split than they would be under the status quo. Had the legislature passed the measure and placed it on the ballot, no doubt voters would have rejected it overwhelmingly.

While my preference would be to distribute in dividends all of those earnings not required for inflation proofing the fund, that would only make sense if we provided means by which some of those dividend dollars, when and if required for essential government services, could be recouped.

The alternative is to permit state government to use prospective dividend dollars as it sees fit. Those legislators who would prefer to so use money now going out in dividends argue that government can spend those funds more efficiently than can individuals. Perhaps true, but hardly more *equitably*. Government services that impact every Alaskan differently are in themselves a form of inequitably dispersed "dividends." To date some $80 billion in nonrecurrent Alaskan oil wealth has been spent largely for recurrent government expenditures such as education and other mandated services. By contrast, not one cent of oil money has gone out in individual dividends—only about half the earnings of that portion of our oil wealth that goes into the Permanent Fund—which now totals at this writing over $30 billion.[1] Certainly, some Alaskans have squandered their dividends, but most have used their dividends to fund their children's higher education or to offset the impact of local taxes and Alaska's high cost of living.

Another Lost Opportunity

Looming large during the 2002 state elections were proposals for bridging Alaska's so-called fiscal gap between recurrent revenues the state takes in and recurrent expenditures. While most candidates ran with assurances that they would address the fiscal gap, when oil prices rose to help bail us out, the issue was virtually abandoned.

Some of us thought instead that then was the easiest time to put in place a contingency plan that would be implemented only if clearly required. In an attempt to devise one, I met with retired State Senator Rick Halford, deemed by many to be one of the most knowledgeable, intelligent, and respected legislators to have ever served the state. We drew up a plan that required a threshold be set beneath which the CBR could

1. Editor's note: "The Alaska Permanent Fund returned 14.5% for the first half of Fiscal Year 2011, and ended December 31 with a value of $38.4 billon." See Alaska Permanent Fund Corporation (online), *Fund News*, February 4, 2011.

not be depleted without triggering means to recoup revenues required to bring it back up to that threshold. This could be accomplished through either budget cuts or increased taxes. If the latter, they would only be imposed to the extent necessary to retain the CBR threshold and then would be suspended or declined accordingly if no longer needed.

I suggested that such an "insurance" plan be called the Halford Plan. He objected saying that appending his name to it would bring excessive political baggage and that it instead be called the Hammond Plan. Not wishing to taint it by appending either of our names to it, we elected to call it the Parachute Plan. Our rationale was that the parachute would only deploy if necessary to assure a soft, rather than the catastrophic, crash landing, which could occur were the CBR no longer able to provide any cushioning and only Permanent Fund money be available to cushion the fall.

When the campaign manager for gubernatorial candidate Frank Murkowski became aware of our plan, he called me to announce, "What a wonderful idea! Frank will love it." When I told him of our debatable choice of names for the plan he said, "We'll call it the Murkowski plan." I told him that would be fine with me.

Meanwhile, Murkowski's opponent, Democratic candidate Fran Ulmer, instantly perceived the wisdom embodied in the Parachute Plan concept and ardently supported it publicly. Fran had worked for me during my administration and so impressed me with her intelligence and dedication that I once offhandedly said if she ever chose to run, she would have my endorsement. Later a newsperson who was aware of that commitment asked me if I intended to keep it despite the fact that when I made it Fran had not declared a political party preference, while I had declared as a Republican. My response was, "Of course."

Supporting her against Republican Murkowski was viewed as apostasy by many Republicans and no doubt helped kill the Parachute Plan that, by now, was being branded the Fran Ulmer Parachute Plan. Unfortunately, in announcing her ardent support for the plan, Ulmer stated that everything would be on the table, including a possible income tax. Once again we saw why so few politicians feel they can afford to be totally honest. It was soon charged that if Fran Ulmer were elected, she would resurrect the income tax. With this, she no doubt lost droves of votes. Had she instead asserted that a whole range of budget cuts would be considered instead of taxes, conservatives would have applauded her.

Rather than permitting Fran Ulmer as governor to impose an income tax upon resentful Alaskans, the Parachute Plan would have *prevented* her from doing so unless conditions were such that most Alaskans agreed some sort of broad-based tax was necessary. Though increasing numbers of Alaskans had already reached that conclusion, the Parachute Plan died aborning.

Later upon his election, Governor Murkowski requested I meet with him. I did so with some trepidation, fearing there might be some residual resentment for my support of his prime opponent. Instead, he was most affable and sought my counsel on several matters.

In conveying that counsel I suggested he at least establish a threshold beneath which he would not permit the CBR to deplete. He agreed and set that threshold at $1.5 billion. At the time it appeared we had about two years before the CBR would drop below $1 billion. Subsequent escalating oil prices, however, have deferred that moment of truth indefinitely before that threshold would be met. Again, despite assertions of virtually every legislative candidate in fall 2004 that "fixing the fiscal gap" would be one of their highest priorities, the flood of new oil wealth sluiced it off the legislative agenda.

When the income tax was passed by the Territorial Legislature and signed into law by Governor Ernest Gruening, it served to save the state from bankruptcy, according to historian Terrence Cole. Yet, as I said, Alaskans, like most Americans, are so anti-tax that should we structure a tax that made them money, as would have my original Bristol Bay, Inc., proposal—most would oppose it. A courageous action by the Alaska House to resurrect an income tax brought voter wrath down upon them and cost some members who supported it their next election. Because of her support, our current U.S. Senator Lisa Murkowski, previously one of the most popular and talented state legislators, almost lost her reelection bid for the State House.[2] Later, during her campaign for the U.S. Senate, charges that she had supported a state income tax were resurrected and no doubt cost her many votes.

2. Editor's note: U.S. Senator Lisa Murkowski was officially named the winner of Alaska's U.S. Senate race on Thursday, December 30, 2010, making history by becoming Alaska's first winning write-in candidate. Paraphrased from *Anchorage Daily News* (adn.com), November 7, 2010.

Governor Murkowski's Fiscal Gap Conference

In February 2004, Governor Frank Murkowski called a conference of some fifty appointed Alaskans to discuss Alaska's "fiscal gap," which for each of the past several years has required use of nonrecurrent revenues to span the difference between recurrent income and recurrent expenditures. A change in my travel plans allowed me to attend. While I had not intended to speak at the conference, a majority of those present insisted I be permitted to do so. At first I declined, but when granted a few hours to prepare remarks I agreed.

While the governor had asked conferees to confine comment to discussion of a percent of market value (POMV), I said I found it impossible to completely isolate discussions of a POMV from the manner in which it, in conjunction with other measures, could help span the fiscal gap with minimal pain. As a guiding principle, I urged conferees to place paramount our constitution's mandate to manage our resources for the maximum benefit of the people. That to me means all our people, not simply the fortunate or recipients of subsidized jobs or state services. Nothing, I said, better meets that mandate than our dividend program. If you dispute that, I challenge you to poll Alaskans and ask what state program provides them with a greater benefit. While perhaps some would list one of our free state services over dividends, those are in effect selective "dividends" that inequitably benefit some Alaskans far more than others.

Reducing dividends to pay for government services would impose what is, in essence, a reversibly graduated "head tax" on all and only Alaskans. The poor would pay a larger percentage of their "income" in taxes than would the rich; transient pipeline workers, commercial fishermen and construction workers would get off scott–free. I suggested that dividends be increased and then recaptured as necessary through either income or sales taxes, or, my favorite, user fees, which charged prime beneficiaries of services in proportion to benefits received. Former State Senator Rick Halford told me he first opposed the dividend program only to become one of its staunchest advocates. Efforts to reduce dividends to permit legislators to spend some of those dollars prompted this comment from Halford: "We Alaskans are like a bunch of Neanderthals who, when confronted with mammoth oil wealth, consumed the bulk of the carcass, spending over $80 billion in the process for things future generations of Alaskans will have long forgotten. Now we are squabbling over the 20 percent of the bones and the bowels still left."

For a long time, I too have feared we would continue to make the same mistakes that Pérez Alfonso, the World Bank, and economist Vernon Smith warned against: investing in new programs and projects when resource wealth is abundant, only to find when oil prices decline we are almost bankrupt and can't maintain them.

The People's Portfolio Plan that Governor Murkowski's conference proposed for Alaska consisted of three parts. First, establish a POMV endowment that would annually disperse 5 percent of the fund's market value in dividends. Second, tax, or assign a user fee, and back money required to fund essential government services. Tie the magnitude of such taxes or user fees to the amount required to keep the Constitutional Budget Reserve at or above the governor's $1.5 billion threshold. Third, make the tax rate flexible so that it is not locked in concrete but could decline or be suspended should other appropriate revenues become available.

While in many ways I personally would prefer a state sales tax, its regressive nature poses problems. As an alternative I suggested an income tax capped at no more than one's dividend, since it appeared to have greater public support. As I had mentioned earlier, this capped income tax concept occurred to me during the 1999 debate on the legislature's proposed fiscal gap plan, which proposed not only a modest income tax but potentially unlimited use of Alaska Permanent Fund money. Thus, I made a dozen or so radio, television, and public presentations.

At one such presentation, a Rotary Club member rose to state: "I don't mind losing my dividend but I'll be damned if I want to be taxed on my hard earned income just to assure the less productive can get theirs."

I asked: "How many of you agree?" Virtually every hand went up.

I then asked: "I can understand that, but what if we were simply to cap the tax at no more than your dividend? You say you don't mind losing yours, but why take it away from who can least afford it?"

His response: "I could live with that."

I again asked: "How many agree?" Again virtually all raised their hands.

I proposed the capped income tax primarily to cut the legs out from under those who oppose a regular income tax for the justifiable reasons that it could penalize productivity and transfer one's hard earned income to those who are less productive. It was suggested in hopes of bolstering support from fainthearted legislators who are intimidated by screams of outrage anytime someone mentions the words "income tax." Certainly, a flat, uncapped income tax would be less regressive, because a tax on capped income, after some time, might begin as a progressively graduated income tax but could dramatically become a regressive tax on more and more Alaskans. If more money were needed, the higher echelon would still pay no more than their dividend, while increasing numbers of less well off Alaskans would begin to pay more than their dividend's worth.

Accordingly, I proposed that the tax cap could only be removed by a vote of the people. While this made it more palatable to some, it posed no great impediment. Alaskans would soon realize they had two choices if more revenue were needed: either remove the cap and capture more revenue from the affluent and less from low-income folk or raise the tax rate percentage to draw in the same number of dollars. Once that knowledge sank in, I suspect that cap would fly off faster than the cap on a bottle of Bud at a ballpark.

Here's an example of how that plan would have worked in 2004. Five percent of the $30 billion market value of the Permanent Fund would yield dividends of roughly $2,365 for every Alaskan. I am told a tax equal to the national average state income tax, which is 5 percent of what one owes in federal taxes, would yield roughly $250,000,000. Were such the case, an individual would have to earn roughly $170,000 in federal taxable income to pay the state $2,365 in taxes. (A taxpayer would pay the feds 33 percent or $47,850 and the state five percent of that or $2,392.) A family of four would have to have income of over $540,000 to owe the state the equivalency of their four dividends totaling $9,460. (They'd pay the feds 35 percent of $540,000, or $189,000, and the state 5 percent = $9,450.) Pretty darn painless! While conferees seemed increasingly intrigued with this approach and 61 percent of them at first voted to reinstall an income tax, politics prevailed and they next voted to simply urge that an income tax "be considered."

Two days after the conference adjourned I could not believe my ears when the chairman of the conference appeared on television to announce: "Hammond's got his figures all wrong. Why, a person earning but $16,000 in federal taxable income would pay a state income tax equal to his dividend." A few days later the *Voice of the Times*, hardly a bastion of Hammond support, did him one better asserting that a person earning only $15,000 would pay the state his entire dividend.

What the newspaper had done was to apply the *federal* tax schedule that would require a citizen earning $16,000 to pay a *federal* income tax at the 15 percent rate (15 percent of $16,000 = $2,400). The taxpayer would pay the state only 5 percent of that, or $120, leaving a balance of $2,365 minus $120, or $2,245 dividend dollars in his or her pocket. It went on to damn the horrifying suggestion that dividends be increased and a capped income tax imposed, which might take more dividend dollars back from the rich than the poor. An outrageous suggestion!

However, the damage was done. Though I urged the chairman and the *Voice of the Times* to acknowledge their mistake publicly, they never did and the subsequent legislature did nothing whatsoever to address the fiscal gap—this despite the fact that virtually all running for office had pronounced that the fiscal gap was their highest priority.

Fiscal concerns, however, were flushed down the tube when high oil prices provided an unanticipated windfall, the entire amount of which the legislature spent in an orgy of politically popular projects. Not one cent went into the Constitutional Budget Reserve, though by law the legislature is required to repay monies borrowed from that account. Instead, an effort was mounted to use some Permanent Fund earnings affecting dividends without approval by public vote.

Converting the Permanent Fund to an Endowment

Currently, roughly one-half the previous five-year average earnings of the Permanent Fund are distributed annually in dividends. Their size is therefore unpredictable and varies from year to year. While this approach adds a bit to stability, avoiding dramatic fluctuations from year-to-year, it poses predictability and administrative problems. As a consequence, the Permanent Fund Board has proposed the fund be converted to an endowment and five percent of the fund's market value appropriated annually. This is common practice for endowments and is based on the assumption that the corpus of the fund will increase by at least 8 percent per year. This allows for inflation proofing the fund by 3 percent annually, which traditionally has been proven adequate to sustain the fund's value.

The Permanent Fund Board further proposed that the 5 percent appropriated be split 50/50, with half going for dividends and half for "essential government services." Governor Frank Murkowski endorsed the endowment concept and with modifications it could be made acceptable. Two major problems must be overcome before the public would support it. First, it must assure that dividends in the future will be no less than they would be under the current system used to determine their size. Second, in the event that a 5 percent appropriation would invade the corpus of the fund, a public vote would be required under current constitutional mandate. Both of these problems could be addressed by statute without amending the constitution. The requisite legislation could simply read: "Up to 5% of the Permanent Fund's market value may be appropriated annually for dividends, provided, however, the legislature may assess up to 40% of this amount for essential government services. The remainder shall be distributed annually in dividends to all qualified Alaskans. In no case, however, shall dividends be less than one-half the previous five-year average earnings of the fund." Were this statutory approach taken, the fund's board would have to determine each year how much of the 5 percent could be appropriated to avoid invasion of the fund's corpus, which otherwise would require a public vote. Accordingly, the cleanest approach would be to simply amend our constitution with the aforementioned constitutional language.

Were that done at this writing when the Permanent Fund contained about $30 billion, 5 percent would have yielded $1.5 billion. A minimum of $900 million would have gone out in dividends and $600 million would have been available for community dividends. At least $300 million of this would have gone to Anchorage, thereby providing, among other things, immense relief from crippling property taxes. Anchorage Mayor Mark Begich told me that property taxes brought $180 million into Anchorage in 2003, so that relief would be substantial.

Accordingly, in exchange for virtually enshrining dividends in the constitution, the use of no more than 40 percent of the money appropriated from the fund for government services might be acceptable, so long as dividends will be no less than under the status quo.

To date, Alaskans have been very leery of the POMV approach since the original proposal would have not only permitted invasion of the fund's corpus without a public vote, but would have reduced dividends in a few years by hundreds of dollars from what they would otherwise be under the status quo.

Best Means of Spanning Alaska's Fiscal Gap

For years I had sought means of spanning the fiscal gap that would be simple, effective, and salable. Though some pieces of the puzzle were evident, it was not until the POMV endowment concept came forward that the last piece fell in place.

An annual payout of 5 percent of the Permanent Fund's market value could span the fiscal gap with little pain, while accomplishing an amazing array of other worthy objectives. Rather than splitting that 5 percent—half for dividends and half for government services—were we to appropriate it for nothing but dividends, with the provision that no more than 40 percent could be assessed by the legislature for essential government services combined with a capped income tax, we could do all of the following:

—Better meet our constitution's mandate to manage resource wealth for the people's maximum benefit. Now only about 2.5 percent of the fund's value goes for that purpose.

—Span a billion dollar fiscal gap the first year alone: 5 percent of the fund's $30 billion market value would yield $1.5 billion in dividends. Since non-Alaskans would pay at least 10 percent or $100 million, Alaskans would only have to pay $900 million, leaving $600 million to be dispersed in dividends.

—Fully fund education.

—Restore municipal revenue sharing.

—Help eliminate uneconomic development by better ensuring that development will pay its own way.

—Encourage healthy development.

—Fulfill the original intent of the dividend program.

—Increase dividend amount predictability.

—Guarantee continuance of dividends.

—Increase size of dividends.

—Ensure initial minimal political pain.

—Enhance re-election of those who support it.

—Impose spending constraints on legislators.

— Require no immediate tax imposition.

—Reduce federal tax drain on dividends.

—Increase economic "bang for the buck" of dividends.

—Narrow the gap between "haves and have-nots."

—Promote local hiring.

—Promote the Cremo plan concept.

—Remove many from welfare.

—Take not one cent of one's hard-earned income in taxes.

—Increase percentage of tax paid by nonresidents.

—Reduce dependency on oil pricing.

—Staunch "brain drain."

—Make Alaska not only the most envied state in the nation but also, as economist Smith asserts, an example for all other oil states or nations.

Most to whom we explained the plan instantly saw its potential and evidenced support. Those who did not were asked to review the plan and disprove our contention it could meet all of the above worthy objectives. So far none has done so. Some, however, still would prefer to use half an endowment's appropriation for government services. They concede, however, that such an approach would never pass voter muster since it would reduce prospective dividends by hundreds of dollars in a few years.

A Broken Bargain

When I was in office, the state, the oil companies, and the federal government agreed to split the oil wealth pie roughly one-third, one-third, one-third. Initially, such was the case. However, in the early 1980s oil interests proposed that an Economic Limit Factor (ELF) be established, which granted oil companies a break for certain declining fields or when oil prices dipped precipitously. I said I would support ELF only if it did not reduce the state's one-third share. Initially it did not. However, not long after I left office, ELF was renegotiated to grant oil companies an even better break in light of oil prices that had plunged to about $10 per barrel. Unfortunately, however, no countering provision assured that should the price climb monumentally, providing a windfall to operators, an amount of that windfall sufficient to rebalance the three-way split arrangement would blow the state's way. Instead, federal legislation granted an additional share of that pie to the oil companies, resulting in 2004 in roughly 19 percent, or $2.28 billion, going to the federal coffers, 27 percent, or $3.24 billion, to the state, and a whopping 53 percent, or $6.35 billion, to the oil companies. As a consequence, the state has been shortchanged hundreds of millions of dollars each year for the past several years and will continue to be denied what was once agreed to be our "fair share."

To Governor Murkowski's credit, in 2005 he proposed at least a modest change in ELF that would recapture some of that loss. Naturally, oil operators heatedly opposed it, suggesting they would pack up their drill bits and leave if readjustments to ELF were carried out. Unfortunately, oil interests contribute substantially to the election of many legislators who seem inclined to bow to oil company threats, rather than place the public interest above that of big oil.

Naturally, oil interests scream in anguish at any proposals that could diminish their percentage of the take, asserting they might leave should we now "change the rules of the game." Of course, when it was to their benefit, they had no hesitation about changing those rules, which subsequently boosted their share far above the initially agreed upon one-third, while reducing the state's share accordingly.

Currently an initiative designed to place the issue before the voters has been proposed and would likely pass in light of the tremendous profits oil companies are gleaning with high oil prices.

Of course, there is a point of diminishing returns when one is dealing with golden geese. At what point does massaging the cloacae to encourage the expulsion of ever more eggs translate into a throttling?

I do not blame the oil companies for opposing changes to ELF. After all, it is the obligation of their CEOs to get the best possible deal for their stockholders. When as governor I was asked how much I would tax oil, my response was: "For every cent we can possibly get. After all, just as it is the obligation of oil company CEOs to maximize benefits for their stockholders, so is it the obligation of the state's CEO to do the same for his." That is where the concept of stock ownership in the Permanent Fund comes in. By granting all Alaskans a share they tend to notice whether or not that share is a fair one and thereby support efforts to assure that development clearly pays its own way—and then some.

Ideally, we should have put all our resource wealth into the Permanent Fund and lived off its earnings. Had we followed the wise counsel of attorney Roger Cremo, who attempted to persuade Governor Keith Miller in 1970 to put all our resource wealth into a Permanent Fund–type investment portfolio, it could now spin off both significantly higher dividends and fund essential government services. Unfortunately, only a handful of legislators agreed.

Since it makes no sense not to provide the means to retrieve some of those dividend dollars through taxes or user fees if needed, I favor the latter, which obligates to the best extent possible those who receive the most benefits from a public service to pay most. For example, if minors receive thousands in dividends and more money is required to fund education, I see no reason why they should not be required to relinquish a portion of their dividends as tuition. After all, education is the state's largest single expenditure and minors are the prime beneficiaries. Curiously, under normal taxing procedures those with fewer children actually pay more for education because of tax exemptions granted parents with several children in school. Charging tuition would help remedy this inequity and imbue children with a sense of responsibility and understanding that services cost money. Similarly, state subsidies for highway and ferry systems could be eliminated were Alaska's gasoline taxes to be raised at least to the national average.

However, first, oil taxes should be adjusted to redeem the state's initially agreed upon one-third share. Only then should user fees or a broad-based sales or income tax be imposed if we lack sufficient revenues to fund essential government programs. Alaska is fortunate in having a clear means of deciding just when and to what degree such taxes might be required.

The World Bank and Others Wade In

For a number of years, other states and nations seemed unaware of the Alaska Permanent Fund and its dividend program. Then, in the spring of 1999, I received four phone calls evidencing growing interest. The first came from a Danish television production crew, which informed me that they were coming to Alaska and wanted to interview me on our Permanent Fund program, in the belief it might have worthy application in

Greenland. They informed me that in the past, development of Greenland's natural resources is perceived to have yielded little benefit to the majority of Greenlanders, while a select few have prospered. They were intrigued with Alaska's program and believed it might have application for new resource development contemplated in Greenland. They wondered if I would permit them to interview me on the matter. I was pleased to do so.

Shortly thereafter I received a call from the World Bank asking if I would be willing to go to Washington to brief its members on the Permanent Fund program. They had looked at every other state and nation with oil wealth and concluded that Alaska had done by far the best job of assuring that all Alaskans receive some benefit. Second, in the bank's view, was Norway, which in large measure copied its program after Alaska's, the difference being that Norway distributes government services such as socialized health care and unemployment benefits rather than cash dividends.

When I appeared before the World Bank, I advised them of efforts in the state to cap or even eliminate the dividend program by some who believe government, rather than the people, should determine how all the oil wealth is spent. Their advice was: "Don't change it. It's a stroke of genius since it provides transparency. Dividend recipients are inclined to view far more clearly what government does with their resource wealth if they have a direct, discernible stake in it such as is provided by dividends."

Echoing Juan Pablo Pérez Alfonso, they informed me that citizens in many oil-rich states and nations found themselves worse off than before. They cited Nigeria as one example. Some $296 billion in oil wealth had flowed through its economy and left in its wake infrastructure and government services that could not be sustained when oil prices or flow declined. While a few prospered handsomely, most citizens ended up saddled with debt rather than discernible benefits. Throw in a heaping helping of corruption and you have a recipe for disaster. Nigerians present confirmed this conclusion and expressed great interest in adopting a program like Alaska's, which to a large degree countered destructive past practices.

I next received a call from a party in British Columbia who wanted to promote an Alaska-type program for that province.

Finally, I received a call advising me of a book entitled *Who Owns the Sky* by one Peter Barnes. The cover blurb states:

Global warming has finally made clear the true costs of using our atmosphere to soak up unwanted by-products of industrial activity. As nations, businesses, and citizens seek workable yet fair solutions for reducing carbon emissions, the question of who should pay—and how—looms large. Yet the surprising truth is that a system for protecting the atmosphere could be devised that would yield cash benefits to us all. In *Who Owns the Sky*, Peter Barnes redefines the debate about the cost and benefits of addressing climate change. He proposes a market-based institution called a "Sky Trust" that would set limits on carbon emissions and pay dividends to all of us who collectively own the atmosphere as a commons. The trust would be funded by requiring polluters to pay for the right to emit carbon dioxide and managed by a nongovernmental agency. Dividends would be paid annually, in much the same way as residents of Alaska today receive cash benefits from oil companies that drill in their state. . . . Barnes sets forth a practical new approach to our shared inheritance—not only the atmosphere, but water, forests and other life-sustaining and economically valuable common resources as well. He shows how we can use markets and property rights, not only to preserve and share from [natural resources], but also to pass [them] on undiminished to future generations.

The Ideal Solution: A Plan for Iraq?

In spring 2004, a *New York Times* article by Steven Clemons advocated a Permanent Fund dividend–type program for Iraq, asserting nothing could do more to promote a democratic capitalistic mind-set among masses of unemployed young Muslims. Were they to sample a bit better life while here, they might be less inclined to seek "paradise" by blowing themselves up along with as many "infidels" as possible.

Every revolution in history—Russian, Chinese, French, and U.S.—was triggered by the gulf between the "haves" and "have-nots." Certainly, Iraq seems fertile ground for another. Under Saddam, those at the top lived in opulence and those at the bottom in squalor. Oil wealth fattened the few, while the many starved. Shunting some of the country's oil wealth to the citizens might do a lot to help forestall further chaos.

Certainly, it would incline most Iraqis to oppose terrorists who were blowing up "their" pipelines and thereby hitting each and every Iraqi directly in the pocketbook.

I sent the *Times* article to Senator Ted Stevens, suggesting he show it to President George W. Bush. Stevens advised he had, and that the President was intrigued. Soon after, Secretary Colin Powell and members of Congress were on television advocating dividends as an Iraqi democratization effort.

Later, I was asked to keynote an address to an international congregation in Washington, D.C., supporting such a plan. Brazilian Senator Eduardo Siplicy introduced me saying, "A few years ago I read this man's book outlining Alaska's dividend program (*Tales of Alaska's Bushrat Governor*). It inspired me to introduce legislation in Brazil. Last year the Governor signed it into law. Brazilians feel it's one of the best things that ever happened."

Economists, educators and others present then stated what they thought to be a dividend plan's potentials, not only for Iraq, but also for their own countries. At conference end, dividend programs had been proposed for Mexico, Chad, Venezuela, Ecuador, and Bolivia, among others.

Dr. Stephen Bezruchka of the University of Washington School of Medicine made an intriguing presentation. He had studied the general health of various nationalities. To his surprise, he found the health of a nation was not nearly so dependent on quality or availability of health care as on the gap between the "haves" and the "have-nots." He cited Japan, which, despite having the highest rate of smoking among developed countries, now ranks number one in the world as far as collective health of its citizens is concerned. In 1960 Japan ranked sixteenth, while the United States ranked thirteenth. What caused the change?

According to Dr. Bezruchka, the United States has the greatest wealth and income gap of any rich country, which is the main explanation for its dismal health ranking among developed countries. As our wealth and income gaps have grown, so has our distance from being the healthiest country. After the Second World War, Japan restructured its economy to be egalitarian. Today, during its economic crisis, managers and chief executive officers are taking cuts in pay rather than laying off workers, something that is inconceivable in the United States.

By contrast, America has continued to drop on that international "health meter" and in 1997 had dropped to No. 25. Bezruchka attributes this to the fact that for the past twenty years every state has seen an *increase* in the gap between "haves" and "have-nots," with one exception. Alaska is the only state in which that gap has narrowed.

His attributing this to dividends at first confused me. After all, both fat and not-so-fat cats get the same dollop of dividend "milk." Why, therefore, would the gap not remain constant? The answer, of course, is now we have almost 200,000 new income recipients, children, added to the equation, boosting those at the lower end.

During my comments to the conference, I mentioned that I had urged U.S. Senator Ted Stevens to advocate an Iraqi dividend program to the President, and I hoped to discuss it with the President personally. Not all conferees were Bush supporters. One complained: "Hey, that might help get Bush re-elected. How about getting together with Kerry instead?" Another asked, "If we can arrange it, would you meet with Nader?" My response was that I would be glad to meet with any candidate. I would love to see them vying to promote what could well be a popular and effective step in offsetting charges no one had a peace plan for Iraq. I was pleased to learn that Senator Lisa Murkowski did introduce a resolution advocating a dividend program for Iraq.

Folk from elsewhere seem far more aware of a dividend program's potentials than many Alaskan politicians who covertly hate it simply because if they can't get their hands directly on those dividend dollars, it compels them to consider cutting budgets or advocating new taxes. Both actions demand intestinal fortitude, seemingly in short supply these days.

At conference end, a professor of economics who had written a book advocating dividends for other states and nations made a comment to the effect that conservatives in Alaska must love the dividend program since it is by far the most conservative thing that could have been done with their oil wealth. It makes a mini-capitalist out of every Alaskan and avoids spending all that oil wealth on government as would socialists. Reflecting on this, it occurred to me that Alaska's shift from a "liberal" Democrat dominance prevailing prior to dividends to the "conservative" Republican stance of the present coincided exactly with advent of the dividend program. I told him that, oddly, it is the so-called Democrat "liberals" who now seem the most ardent defenders of dividends. He found this as perplexing as do I.

In an article appearing in the *Wall Street Journal* in 2003, Nobel laureate for economics Vernon Smith had this to say about Alaska's Permanent Fund dividend and its possible implication for oil-rich countries such as Iraq:

> With the capture of Saddam Hussein, President Bush has a symbolic victory against his critics. However, the unfinished Iraqi economic reconstruction presents the President with a historic opportunity to craft a new geopolitical economic paradigm for movement of assets from governments to citizens.
> The last decades have seen a world-wide transfer of state owned assets to private entities, most often as governments have found themselves unable to afford their varying brands of socialism.
> However, this transfer of assets has served largely to generate funds for government—sales to retire government debt, fund political priorities, or as an alternative for raising taxes—creating a funding system easier for politicians but more difficult for the public it serves.
> For long-term success, the enormous task of nation rebuilding in Iraq requires attention to more than the creation of a political democracy. No matter how well intentioned a democracy might be, the next government will be tempted to corruption, violation power if it owns and controls the great economic wealth potential of Iraq. This is the time, and Iraq is the place, to create an economic system embracing the revolutionary principle that public assets belong directly to the public—and can be managed to further individual benefit and free choice, without intermediate government ownership in the public name.
> There is a very important precedent, in part for this action—The Alaska Permanent Fund. The State of Alaska elected to put a portion of its vast Prudhoe Bay annual royalty revenue into a citizens' Permanent Fund for investment in securities. Each year a dividend from this Fund is dispersed to every Alaskan citizen. This Fund was the first to recognize the full rights of citizens to share directly in the income from public assets.

This Fund, however, has important shortcomings which should
not be repeated in Iraq.

Smith believes those shortcomings include failure to put *all* our state
revenue from oil wealth into the people's account and using its earning
for nothing but dividends. Instead most of it went to state government.
Says Smith: "When oil prices went up, the state succumbed to the temptation to repeal its income tax and spent its oil income like there was no
tomorrow. Consequently, today the Alaska state government has a
budget crisis and a deficit gap, but the 600,000 Alaska citizens share
equally in dividends from their Fund, now worth $27 billion."[3]
Smith believes that because it disciplines government spending and
the political process, we should require politicians to tax dividend dollars back through what he terms "the eye of the needle of voter
scrutiny." Far better that than to let politicians have free priority access
to what should be the people's earnings on their assets. Smith's article
continues:

> This action would launch the new Iraqi state as one based on
> individual human rights, and the rule of law, and anoint it with
> rock-hard credibility by giving every citizen a stake in that new
> regime of political and economic freedom. The objective is to
> undermine any citizen sense of disenfranchisement in the
> country's wealth, economic and political future, and to
> galvanize citizen support for a democratic regime. Now is the
> time to act, before post war business-as-usual creates de facto
> foreign and domestic spoils of war property rights claims,
> leaving out a citizenry brutalized by a totalitarian regime and in
> sore need of empowerment in their own future.

Afterword by Lauren Stanford

Every morning my grandfather would sip his coffee and solve his cryp-
toquote or crossword at the dining room table of his Lake Clark cabin,
the old radio wheezing nearby. After the last letter was filled in the

3. Editor's note: As of July 2011, it is worth $41 billion.

appropriate box, he would slowly rise from his chair, grasp his cane, and make his way out to his office. His desk and computer were situated among my grandmother's geraniums and achimenes in the solarium. In this little Eden he would perform mundane tasks, then open a document and start typing his numerous thoughts. His final project was *Diapering the Devil*. Ever adamant about protecting and promoting the Alaska Permanent Fund, my grandfather would talk anyone's ear off who would listen. On August 2, 2005, he passed away in his sleep, his voice seemingly silenced forever. Now, due to the hard work and persistence of Larry Smith and others, Jay Hammond will continue to be heard.

3

The Alaska Permanent Fund Dividend: A Case Study in the Direct Distribution of Resource Rent

SCOTT GOLDSMITH

Introduction: Some Background on Alaska

Alaska is the largest of the fifty United States measured by land area—but its 700,000 residents make it one of the smallest in population. Because of Alaska's small population, remote location astride the Arctic Circle, and distance from markets, economic development prospects are limited primarily to exploiting natural resources and federal spending. Most of its economic growth since becoming a state in 1959 has come from petroleum production, which alone accounts for a third of all jobs, directly and indirectly.

The economic history of Alaska before statehood was one of periodic resource-driven booms—furs, gold, copper, timber, and fish—followed by busts due to resource depletion or market conditions. Each boom generated substantial income, but most went to nonresidents who left behind little to benefit permanent ones. Many residents felt the policies of the federal government were stifling growth and advocated for greater local control.

When Alaska became a state, its government took title to about 24 percent of the land and adopted a constitution specifically requiring management of public resources for the maximum benefit of its people.

Reprinted with permission of Revenue Watch Institute

The idea of Alaska as the "Owner State," where the wealth from natural resources formed the economic base and was shared by all residents, was promoted by one of the early governors, Wally Hickel.

Alaska's economy was initially weak, but in 1968 the largest oil field on the continent was discovered on state land at Prudhoe Bay in the northernmost part of the state, a region called the North Slope. In 1977 production began; since then the state economy has been dominated by petroleum production and the revenues it has generated.

The direct contribution of North Slope petroleum production to gross state product has varied between 9 and 50 percent (table A) with the annual variation attributable primarily to petroleum production and price. The $149 billion (2010 $) in direct petroleum revenues (taxes and royalties) has allowed taxes on other industries to be kept low and on households to be eliminated.[1] At the same time state government spending has expanded to a level twice that of the rest of the nation on a per capita basis.

About 25 percent of direct petroleum revenues have been deposited into two savings accounts—the Alaska Permanent Fund and the smaller Constitutional Budget Reserve. The earnings on these accounts and the remaining direct petroleum revenues together have accounted for 92 percent of total state revenues (excluding federal transfers). And 89 percent of total state spending has come from these direct petroleum revenues and earnings on savings accounts.

Largely because of the windfall from petroleum, the state economy—measured by per capita income and the unemployment rate—has been strong since the 1970s. However, these statewide average economic indicators mask important regional differences in economic performance. In particular, the remote rural part of the state that is inaccessible by road is burdened with high costs and few employment opportunities in the cash economy. About half of the Native Alaskan population lives in this region; they have little cash income and rely primarily on government assistance and subsistence harvesting of fish and game.

Two outside interests continue to be important in the economy: the federal government and the large oil companies that have leased and developed the oil fields. Both are perceived often to work at cross-purposes with state interests, and thus their presence fosters the notion that the state must continue the struggle to take control of its economic future. The shared public ownership of the natural resource wealth of the state is a vehicle to accomplish that goal.

Origins and Evolution of the Alaska Permanent Fund

In its first decade as a state, Alaska had a small tax base in relation to its public needs and struggled to pay its bills. Subsequent to the discovery of oil at Prudhoe Bay, the lease sale generated $900 million for the state treasury—a bonanza compared with the $128 million annual budget at that time. Government spending increased in anticipation of the petroleum revenues that would come with production, but construction of a pipeline to take the oil to market was delayed. Before production revenues began to flow in 1977 into the treasury, the state had spent the entire bonus and was essentially forced to borrow from the oil companies against the future revenues they would be paying.[2]

This experience was an important lesson for Alaskans. When oil had been discovered, the idea of a savings account was discussed at a series of citizen conferences sponsored by the Alaska legislature. People were motivated by the realization that the state was suddenly wealthy beyond belief. The Prudhoe Bay field was an "elephant" in the language of petroleum geologists—clearly a once-in-a-lifetime opportunity. There was almost no likelihood of additional discoveries of that size, so the production and revenues from the North Slope would be a temporary phenomenon. The question was how to convert that windfall into sustainable economic prosperity.

The consensus before that time was that a savings account should be established after production began and that the lease sale bonanza could be better spent on infrastructure development. However, the rapid disappearance of that bonanza, whether it was actually well spent or squandered, convinced most Alaskans of the need for a savings account. It would be the only way to keep some of the oil revenues away from a profligate legislature and preserve some of the petroleum wealth for future generations.

Some people argued against the idea of a public savings account, either on ideological or practical grounds. One argument was that saving was not an appropriate government function, but instead should be left to the private sector. This view, however, ignored the problem with

TABLE A. Alaska Petroleum Production, Revenues, and Savings

Nominal millions of dollars

Year	Gross state product		State petroleum revenues			Permanent Fund deposits[a]		Constitutional Budget Reserve (CBR) deposits[b]
	Total	Petroleum production	Total	Taxes	Royalties	Royalties	Special contributions	Total
1977	7,492	831	482	168	314	4	0	—
1978	9,088	1,616	492	289	203	51	0	—
1979	10,863	2,234	906	570	336	84	0	—
1980	15,138	5,939	2,601	1,223	1,378	344	0	—
1981	21,665	10,801	3,689	2,173	1,516	385	900	—
1982	23,348	10,469	3,975	2,393	1,582	401	800	—
1983	22,548	8,352	3,448	1,882	1,565	421	400	—
1984	23,829	8,785	3,228	1,789	1,439	366	300	—
1985	26,219	10,572	3,116	1,686	1,425	368	300	—
1986	18,849	4,345	2,981	1,355	1,626	323	0	—
1987	22,258	7,948	1,565	871	694	171	1,264	—
1988	21,307	7,113	2,368	1,073	1,295	418	0	—
1989	23,357	7,799	2,069	955	1,114	228	0	—
1990	24,987	8,483	2,388	1,209	1,180	267	0	—
1991	22,164	5,514	3,297	1,554	1,743	435	0	291

1992	22,591	5,321	2,592	1,288	1,305	338	0	247
1993	22,965	4,849	3,197	1,202	1,995	315	0	914
1994	23,110	4,336	1,939	771	1,168	210	0	437
1995	24,805	5,432	3,478	980	2,499	318	0	1,543
1996	26,083	6,984	2,514	1,017	1,498	264	1,842	586
1997	25,171	5,035	2,889	1,245	1,644	308	803	570
1998	23,312	2,699	1,906	829	1,077	231	0	343
1999	23,866	2,682	1,119	565	554	156	0	50
2000	25,913	3,901	2,402	910	1,491	311	280	448
2001	27,747	3,450	2,274	1,087	1,187	339	7	49
2002	28,887	3,947	1,671	724	994	258	0	90
2003	30,905	4,511	2,059	799	1,261	398	0	22
2004	34,408	6,174	2,430	998	1,432	368	0	8
2005	37,824	7,820	3,357	1,430	1,928	481	0	27
2006	41,820	9,919	4,344	1,915	2,429	601	0	44
2007	44,288	10,365	5,115	2,868	2,246	532	0	101
2008	48,551	13,288	11,239	7,510	3,729	844	0	438
2009	45,709	n.a.	5,954	3,715	2,239	651	0	122
2010	n.a.	n.a.	6,105	3,438	2,667	679	0	510

Sources: U.S. Department of Commerce, Alaska Department of Revenue, Alaska Permanent Fund Corp. All data are fiscal year except gross state product.

a. Permanent Fund deposits shown here do not include inflation proofing.

b. CBR deposits begin in 1991 and come from petroleum revenues obtained through settlement of disputes with taxpayers.

purely private savings. Alaska's population was the most transient in the nation. Future generations of Alaskans would be unlikely to benefit from the private savings of current residents. Another problem was whether there was enough petroleum to ensure the continuity of the state's economic development. Under a scenario of continuously growing prosperity, saving would be a mistake.

The question was put to a vote in 1976, and voters approved the creation of the Alaska Permanent Fund by a two-to-one margin.[3] Capitalization would come from deposits of at least 25 percent of the mineral royalties collected on state lands. The fund would invest in income-producing assets. Earnings could be spent, but the principal would be permanently protected. All other details about the fund were left to the legislature to work out.

The most important of those details were the contribution rate, investment philosophy, management structure, and disposition of earnings. All were decided openly in legislative hearings after public discussions throughout the state.

The choice of the contribution rate was important because putting aside too little would not guarantee benefits for future generations, while saving too much would underfund the needs of the current generation. The legislature generally followed the guideline established in the language of the vote in depositing 25 percent of royalties into the fund.[4] Occasionally it has added to the fund balance with special contributions, motivated both by a desire to save more and to reduce the temptation of future legislatures to overspend any current surplus. However, there has never been a formal determination of a target amount that should be saved in order to balance current against future needs.

The question of investment philosophy was a protracted debate over whether the fund should be a development fund or a savings account. Those who preferred the latter ultimately won.

A development fund would have invested in projects designed to strengthen and diversify the economy, so when Alaska no longer had an economic base from oil, other sectors would be strong enough to take its place. Supporters of this position argued that there were many projects that could help the state economy grow, but they could not secure financing either because the capital market was not working due to remoteness and the small size of the economy, or because some projects required a capital subsidy in order to move forward. In either case, they argued, the Permanent Fund would be the vehicle to concentrate the state's efforts to build a more diversified economy through investments in public infrastructure, industrial development, and housing. They further maintained that a portfolio of bonds and stocks would not generate benefits for Alaskans.

Proponents of the savings account approach argued that investing in a portfolio of financial assets not directly linked to the Alaskan economy would maximize the fund's long-term financial earnings and that those earnings would then be available to the state for any purpose in the future. Investing outside the state would diversify Alaska's overall economic portfolio—an important consideration for an economy with a history of cycles of boom and bust. They believed that a state development fund would be driven by political rather than economic decisions. Basing investment choices on politics would produce neither a positive financial return for the state nor a strong portfolio of investments.

The fund was initially managed within the Department of Revenue with other state funds until the legislature established an independent state corporation, the Permanent Fund Corp., to manage the fund portfolio. The corporation is insulated from but not independent of the other branches of government. The governor appoints the six members of the board of trustees who set fund policy, and the director oversees the investments. The corporation's mission is clearly defined to be financial management. It has no role in determining how fund income is to be used.

The constitutional amendment creating the fund gave the legislature authority to spend fund income consisting of interest, dividends, and realized capital gains, but the fund itself must be preserved. In practice this has been interpreted to mean that the inflation-adjusted value of the cumulative deposits into the fund must be preserved.[5] This is accomplished through "inflation proofing," which means depositing a portion of income back into the fund each year to preserve its value.[6]

In practice the corporation has retained fund income until it's been appropriated by the legislature. This separate account is a contingency fund that can be used to supplement current year earnings to pay inflation proofing or the Permanent Fund dividend if current year earnings should fall short.[7] Keeping this accumulated income with the corporation has also protected it from appropriation by the legislature for other purposes.

The most significant change in the structure and management of the Permanent Fund since its formative years has been the liberalization of its investment policy to maximize its potential for long-term growth. Over time the board has asked for and received permission from the legislature on several occasions to expand the categories of investments that the portfolio could hold, as well as to adjust the target range for the allocation among different categories of investments. The fund portfolio now invests globally in stocks, bonds, real estate, and private equities. The investment policy is the "prudent investor" rule: this means that "the corporation shall exercise the judgment and care under the circumstances then prevailing that an institutional investor of ordinary prudence, discretion and intelligence exercises in the designation and management of large investments entrusted to it."[8]

This has increased the volatility in annual realized income. A recent suggestion to manage the fund like an endowment would reduce this volatility, automatically protect it against inflation, and provide more flexibility for management of the fund portfolio. Even though the corporation supports this change, it has not been adopted, largely because the public views any change in the fund's management as an attack on the Permanent Fund dividend.[9]

By 2010 the fund had grown to $32 billion (table B). Of this, $12 billion had come from required royalty deposits, $7 billion from occasional special contributions, and $13 billion from inflation proofing. During its lifetime the fund has averaged a total return of 8.7 percent and has generated realized income of $35 billion. About half of this has been used to pay the Permanent Fund dividend. The rest has either been put back into the fund as inflation proofing or retained in the contingency account.

Accounting for the Success of the Permanent Fund

The Permanent Fund has successfully transformed a portion of state unsustainable petroleum revenues into a sustainable financial asset that can produce an annual flow of income for future generations of Alaskans. In doing so, it has also helped constrain the growth of public spending and moderated the economic cycles generated by price-sensitive, fluctuating oil revenues. Although the ultimate success of the fund depends on its role in Alaska's transition to a post-petroleum economy, its current success can be attributed to a number of factors.

First, the fund was created in the wake of a constitutional referendum as a separate institution with the sole purpose of managing the financial windfall. There was strong support behind its purpose—to prevent wasteful spending and conserve the resource—and that purpose was not complicated by having the fund address two politically complex issues: the collection of revenues and the use of income. In practice, the dedicated royalty deposits have been like an automatic payroll deduction placed into a retirement account that has grown in value over time.

The fund has not been involved in the management of the state's petroleum wealth. The laws governing petroleum taxes are written by the legislature, and both the negotiations over royalties (governed by contracts between the state and lessee) and the collection of petroleum revenues are the responsibility of various departments within the government.

Differing opinions about the optimal tax rates and royalty terms that could maximize benefits to the state result in constant attempts by both industry and state government to make adjustments. The fund is not involved in these disputes. They center on the fair share of revenues that should go to the state rather than the appropriate amount of revenue to fund particular state programs. These disputes have resulted in several significant changes in tax policy over the years.

Nor is the fund involved in estimating the value of production that is the basis for the calculation of taxes and royalties. Differences of opinion on these often end up being litigated in court.

While there have been cases of corruption involving the bribery of legislators in an attempt to influence petroleum taxes and other legislation impacting the industry, the fund has been insulated from them since it is not involved in setting tax policy.

The fund has also been insulated from the politically charged issue of determining how to use income. This has left the fund's managers free to concentrate on their job, and it has been easy to evaluate their performance.

This institutional structure is different from that of two other petroleum funds against which Alaska is often compared. Both the Norwegian Government Pension Fund and the Alberta Heritage Savings Trust Fund are more closely integrated into the annual budget-making process. In the case of the former, all petroleum revenues are deposited into the fund, and Parliament finances the annual budget. Although that model has worked well in Norway, it is hard to imagine this structure

TABLE B. Alaska Savings Accounts and Permanent Fund Dividend
Nominal dollars

Year	Savings account balances (million $)[a]		Disposition of Permanent Fund earnings[b] (million $)				Permanent fund dividend[a]	
	Constitutional Budget Reserve (CBR)[c]	Permanent Fund balance	Total	Dividend payout	Inflation proofing	Residual[d]	Individual dividend amount ($)	Per capita income ($)
1977	—							12,388
1978	—	53	2			2		12,495
1979	—	137	8			8		13,199
1980	—	483	32			32		14,975
1981	—	1,715	150			150		16,528
1982	—	2,939	368			364	1,000	18,819
1983	—	4,061	471	64	231	176	386	18,843
1984	—	4,548	530	175	151	204	331	19,395
1985	—	6,085	658	217	235	206	404	20,104
1986	—	7,097	1,021	303	216	501	556	19,673
1987	—	8,338	1,069	391	148	529	708	19,244
1988	—	8,757	789	424	303	62	827	19,848
1989	—	9,723	869	460	360	48	873	21,525
1990	—	10,389	916	488	454	(26)	953	22,594
1991	297	11,433	1,031	490	559	(18)	931	23,092
1992	563	12,405	1,036	488	477	71	916	23,706

1993	685	13,748	1,226	532	363	332	949	24,478
1994	614	13,492	1,098	556	372	170	984	25,186
1995	1,994	15,146	1,013	565	348	100	990	25,778
1996	2,518	18,276	1,814	643	407	764	1,130	26,179
1997	3,172	21,095	2,061	747	486	829	1,297	27,197
1998	3,559	22,451	2,595	893	423	1,279	1,541	27,943
1999	2,628	22,500	2,544	1,045	288	1,211	1,770	28,538
2000	2,734	23,544	2,260	1,172	423	665	1,963	30,531
2001	2,995	22,430	1,199	1,113	686	(600)	1,850	32,266
2002	2,469	22,389	257	926	602	(1,271)	1,541	33,144
2003	2,093	24,094	355	691	352	(688)	1,108	33,519
2004	2,164	26,541	1,525	581	524	420	920	34,867
2005	2,236	28,522	1,781	532	641	608	846	36,764
2006	2,267	30,325	2,726	689	856	1,182	1,107	38,839
2007	2,548	33,695	3,471	1,022	860	1,589	1,654	41,081
2008	5,601	30,913	2,971	1,293	808	870	2,069	43,922
2009	7,115	29,496	(2,509)	875	1,143	(4,528)	1,305	42,603
2010	8,664	32,045	1,611	858	0	753	1,281	n.a.

Sources: Alaska Department of Revenue, Permanent Fund Corp., U.S. Department of Commerce. All data are fiscal year except dividend amount and personal income.

a. The first dividend in 1982 was not paid from fund earnings. The 2008 dividend included a special, one-time $1,200 appropriation from the state general fund to offset the high cost of fuel in Alaska caused by the rapid increase in world oil prices.

b. Permanent Fund earnings are the sum of interest, dividends, and realized capital gains. Earnings fund the dividend and the Permanent Fund's inflation proofing. There was no inflation proofing in 2010 because it was funded in advance in 2009.

c. The CBR balance fluctuates due to loans to and repayments from the state general fund to finance ongoing government operations.

d. The residual, if positive, accumulates in a contingency fund (Earnings Reserve). If negative, funds are drawn from the contingency fund to finance the dividend and inflation proofing.

would maintain fiscal discipline, given the political environment in Alaska where the government is continuously expected to stimulate economic development.

The Alberta fund was created by legislative action and originally had four goals: to provide savings for the future, to reduce the government debt load, to improve the quality of life in the province, and to strengthen and diversify the economy. A decade later it was clear that this multipronged approach was not working. So the fund has adopted a clearer focus on financial return.[10]

Second, Alaska has collected more oil revenues than originally expected and has taken advantage of the occasions when revenues were high to create some programs that have diffused potential pressure to spend the Permanent Fund's earnings more broadly. The petroleum revenue stream dedicated to the fund—25 percent of royalties—is only about 10 percent of total annual petroleum revenues (including taxes). This has left 90 percent for the legislature and governor to spend on reducing taxes for businesses and households and for expanding programs. Shortly after the fund was created, petroleum revenues increased dramatically. This allowed for establishing and funding of a number of agencies designed to promote economic development in the state, including the Alaska Renewable Resources Corp., Alaska Industrial Development and Export Authority (AIDEA), the Alaska Housing Finance Corp. (AHFC), the Alaska Science and Technology Foundation, the Alaska Energy Authority, and the Alaska Aerospace Development Corp. These agencies relieved pressure on the Permanent Fund to serve as the development bank.

Some time later a new surge in revenues allowed the state to establish another fund, the Constitutional Budget Reserve, for the purpose of buffering government spending against annual fluctuations in petroleum revenues. The state can borrow from this reserve when revenues are down, but it is required to pay the money back when revenues are high. Like the Permanent Fund, the $9 billion in this account represents petroleum revenues saved.

Third, there is a continuing perception that the state squandered its original bonanza—the $900 million in bonuses collected in 1968. The general consensus was that the best way to avoid that mistake again was to put any new windfalls into the Permanent Fund, where they would be safe from wasteful spending. Over time $7 billion has been added to the fund through special deposits motivated by the desire to get the money "off the table," or unavailable for spending by the government of the day. This impulse has been amplified by a strong general underlying desire to control government operations spending and to avoid the necessity of imposing taxes.

Taken together, the two types of deposits that go into the Permanent Fund (those constitutionally required from royalties and those from windfalls) and payments to the Constitutional Budget Reserve amount to 25 percent of direct petroleum revenues collected since North Slope production began.

Fourth, the fund has a policy of not investing in Alaska. It looks worldwide to build a portfolio to maximize long-term return on investment adjusted for risk. By doing so, the fund avoids any political pressure to funnel money into particular investments favored by powerful individuals or groups or to invest in local projects that produce a non-monetary benefit instead of a financial return.

Fifth, the fund and the corporation are probably the most highly respected institutions in the state. This partly stems from the fact that many of Alaska's most respected leaders, like former Governor Jay Hammond, helped guide the formation of the fund and have continued to advocate for it. The fund has been fortunate to have on the board many members perceived to be farsighted, responsible custodians, such as banker Elmer Rasmuson, who was the first chairman. It has also been able to attract high-quality staff, both from within and outside the state, beginning with the first executive director, Dave Rose.

The transparency of the corporation's operations is evident in numerous ways. Board meetings are open to the public and held in communities throughout the state. The corporation publishes a clearly written annual report, produces educational materials for Alaskans, and maintains a speaker's bureau. One can access a current list of portfolio holdings on a daily basis, the value of the fund, and detailed minutes of past board meetings from the corporation website.[11] It reports annually to the legislature. Finally, because Alaska's population is small, the board members are widely known in their communities.

As a result, the public has a high degree of confidence that the fund is being well managed. Second-guessing the investment decisions of the corporation is not a popular pastime even when the market is down. The public has concentrated on the issue of how to collect the fair share of petroleum wealth from the companies producing oil in the state. Once the wealth has been converted to financial assets, the public feels confident that these assets will be professionally managed for its benefit.

And finally, the Permanent Fund dividend that each citizen receives has created a constituency that protects the fund. Although setting aside some petroleum revenues for the future makes sense and was easy to understand at the time of the original windfall, it has since become harder to support for several reasons. First, it is hard to convince people to save for a future that does not involve them. Alaska's population is quite transient. If a current resident thinks he or she might move away in the future, or even sees neighbors replaced by someone new from another state, he or she is less likely to want to save for the future and more likely to want to spend the wealth today. Second, it is hard to educate new residents who have no experience of Alaska before the windfall about the need to save. An entity with closed borders, such as Norway, does not have this problem to the same degree.

In addition, it is tempting to spend when there is a big pot of cash that appears to be sitting idle and not benefiting the public. Such an environment encourages an infinite number of suggestions for ways to "put that money to work." Some will be good and some not so good, but they will be endless and the pressure to spend will be relentless.

One could argue that the fund would not have survived without the dividend. It is hard to see how the fund would have grown to its current size without the protection it has gotten from its constituency, although the state has established other savings accounts—most notably the Constitutional Budget Reserve. Alaska probably would still have a fund without the dividend, but it would be much smaller.

Origin and Evolution of the Permanent Fund Dividend

In the fund's early years, the annual earnings were small and attracted little attention. Then in 1979 the price of oil increased dramatically as a result of the Iranian revolution, and Alaska's oil revenues quadrupled.

The higher oil price was expected to be permanent, and the legislature began the task of spending all these new revenues. Personal income tax was eliminated and the operating and capital budgets increased. Several new state agencies were established, as were a number of loan programs benefiting businesses and households.

The distribution of all this new wealth was reminiscent of the earlier experience of the wasteful spending of the lease bonus windfall. Furthermore, the benefits from the elimination of taxes, the increased spending, the new agencies, and the loan programs all targeted particular groups or businesses. Many felt that the government was spending recklessly and that the benefits of the spending were not distributed equitably across the population.

Against this background the question of what to do with the income from the Permanent Fund was debated in the legislature. The governor at the time, Jay Hammond, had been a commercial fisherman in a small village in rural Alaska. He had seen how the benefits from harvesting a publicly owned resource were inequitably distributed and went mostly to nonresidents. So he proposed an annual cash distribution to all citizens as a means of ensuring that everyone benefited from oil production on state-owned lands.

His original proposal, put forward in 1980 and known as "Alaska Inc.," was to pay every eligible Alaskan an annual dividend based on length of residency up to a maximum of twenty-five years. That feature was designed to help stabilize the transient population, reward longevity, and minimize dividend-related migration.[12]

The arguments in favor of the program included the notion that individuals knew how to spend money for their own benefit better than politicians and that the dividend would control the growth of the public sector. Overexpansion of government would be bad for the economy after the oil revenues ran out.

Those who argued against the program contended it was in the state's best interest to decide communally how the money would be spent, presumably on public goods such as infrastructure and loan programs. That would stimulate economic development. Others felt that a large portion of the money would be wasted and were particularly concerned with how people receiving "free money," particularly those with low incomes, would respond. Some felt there might be a backlash nationally against Alaska if the state was seen as giving away money.

The dividend faced a battle in the legislature, partly because it did not have a strong constituency or organized interest group to support it politically as did loan programs and capital expenditures. Despite this, Alaska Inc. did pass.

It then was ruled unconstitutional because it did not conform to the equal treatment clause of the U.S. Constitution. Anticipating this ruling, the legislature passed the current dividend plan that paid each qualified Alaska resident regardless of age an equal amount out of the earnings of the Alaska Permanent Fund. The only requirement for eligibility is one year of residency in the state prior to the payment year and the intent to remain a resident in the future. Typically about 95 percent of the population, including children, receives the dividend in the last quarter of the year, about six months after submitting an application establishing residency under the rules of the program.

The amount available for the dividend each year is half of the nominal fund earnings averaged over the previous five-year period.[13] As the Permanent Fund has grown, the dividend has increased in size, although it has fluctuated considerably in size from year to year.[14] In 2010 it represented a 3 percent increment to per capita personal income for the average resident.[15]

The annual aggregate dividend distribution is significant in relation to other sources of income that enter the economy. The $858 million in 2010 is half as big as the entire payroll of the mining and petroleum sectors ($1.664 billion). Since the dividend income comes from nonpetroleum-related investments made outside the state, it is like adding a new basic industry to the economy. This diversification of income sources acts as a stabilizing force on the economy.

After the initial dividend distribution, researchers at the University of Alaska did a comprehensive study of its impact and public attitudes about it to help determine whether to continue the program. Sixty percent of Alaskans surveyed thought the dividend was a good idea, 29 percent had mixed feelings, and 10 percent thought it was a bad idea. (One percent did not know.) When asked to compare the dividend with alternative uses of the funds, respondents preferred uses that distributed funds to households over public construction or more savings. Respondents were overwhelmingly in favor of inflation proofing.[16]

Every subsequent survey has confirmed the overwhelming, but not universal, popularity of the program. For example, a nonrandom survey in 1989 found only 15 percent of respondents were willing to increase state revenues by eliminating the dividend. Somewhat larger percentages were willing to put a cap on its size or spend funds in the contingency account.[17]

Although the Permanent Fund balance, which ultimately determines the size of the dividend, is constitutionally protected, there is no such guarantee for the earnings or the dividend. The legislature has the authority to change the formula at any time and could, by law, eliminate it entirely. Its only guarantee is its political popularity. No legislator would suggest a change in the formula that would reduce its amount or the share of Permanent Fund income allocated to the dividend for fear of losing the next and all subsequent elections.

The dividend also instantaneously created a constituency—the voters—for the Permanent Fund itself. Without a group keeping an eye on the legislature, the fund could have fallen prey to special interests. Such interests might spend the earnings inappropriately, invest the fund's balance in capital projects with no financial return, or eliminate inflation proofing.

The best example of how sensitive the legislature has become to the appearance of reducing the dividend is the special legislative contributions that have been deposited into the fund over the years. These increase the balance of the fund, future income, and with it, the size of the dividend in future years. Legislators are willing to make these special contributions even though they reduce the amount of money they could spend to satisfy special constituencies. It is ironic that the legislature has willingly contributed to a fund established specifically to protect against wasteful legislative spending.

The basic structure of the dividend program has not changed since it was introduced. Changes have involved better definition of eligibility (length of residence and intent to remain) and the streamlining of the payment method. Originally people received the annual payment in the mail, a process that took several weeks. Now most dividends are paid electronically directly into recipients' bank accounts, all on the same day.

Policies have also been established to deal with special situations. For example, certain federal aid programs for low-income families are contingent on monthly income. To offset loss of aid income to those families when they receive their dividend, the state instituted a "hold harmless" program. This is a payment to those families in compensation for their temporary loss of federal assistance. The state also acts as trustee for children who are wards of the state, managing their dividends until they reach adulthood.

When the annual dividend payment is distributed, retailers compete to lure recipients to spend as much of their checks as possible. The local media attention concentrating on the story about how people spend their dividends also contributes to a "consumption-frenzy" atmosphere. This could be part of the source of the wasteful spending cited by some dividend critics.

The distribution method could be structured in any number of ways, but there has been little interest in changing it. The dividend could be accompanied by information on good consumer spending habits or how to use the dividend to better manage consumer debt. The dividend could be distributed on a monthly basis.

The presentation of the dividend could also be framed in a way that guides consumer decisions in a particular direction. The current method does not offer many saving alternatives for recipients either at the time of application or of distribution. Since 1991 applicants have been able to designate part of their dividend to a University of Alaska Section 529 College Savings Plan established to benefit a child. Money earned through the plan is tax free under current law, and the proceeds can be used to pay qualified expenses at the University of Alaska or any other eligible institution of higher learning. To date there have been about 80,000 individual deposits into these accounts via petroleum fund dividend applications. In addition, the "pick-click-give" program, begun in 2009, allows applicants to direct a portion of their dividend to charitable organizations. About 5,000 people used the program in its first year and an estimated 10,000 in 2010.

There has never been a policy discussion of what the best framing structure would be and whether it should include other options for investing or creating a "grubstake"—a means to allow a person to accumulate enough cash for a special opportunity, like starting a business. This is probably because of the feeling among the public that the decision about how the dividend is spent is not the government's business.

A large share of dividends goes to children, and there are no special conditions associated with these payments. In the University of Alaska study, about half of the households that included children reported that the decision about how the children's dividends would be spent was shared between the child and the parent. In the other half, the parents alone made the decision. While parents certainly should be responsible for the well-being of their children, one must wonder if children spending dividend checks is a sensible public policy either in terms of the benefits the children get from those expenditures or from the lessons the children learn about responsible financial management from the experience. There seems to be a good case for weaving some personal finance education into the school curriculum when the dividend is distributed.

Dividend recipients are not required to participate in any community functions like voting, attending community meetings, or even being knowledgeable about the source of the funds they are receiving. The application process could be expanded to provide an education function so people would have a better understanding of why the dividend was established and what it means. It could also be used to informally engage the public to think about important public policy issues.

Public Attitudes toward the Dividend

The dividend has broad but not universal public support. The most frequently heard arguments in its favor are as follows:

—Since the Permanent Fund consists of royalty payments from oil owned by the state, the earnings rightfully belong to the citizens of the state.

—Individuals can put the earnings to better use than allowing the government to decide how to spend the money.

—The dividend is the most equitable way to distribute the benefits from the production of state-owned resources.

—The dividend is a major economic stimulus for the economy (large economic multiplier).

—Without the dividend, the balance of economic activity would be weighted too heavily in favor of the public sector.

—Ending the program would be regressive; it would hurt poor families proportionately more than well-to-do families.

—The dividend protects against a raid on the Permanent Fund.

—The dividend is spent on basic needs of Alaskan families.

—The dividend keeps most of the dollars within the state.

—The dividend is a stabilizing force for the economy otherwise subject to resource-generated cycles.

—The dividend levels the income distribution in the state.

—Life in Alaska is tough. I deserve it.

—I pay Alaska taxes. I should get something back.

Support for the program has certainly been bolstered by the increase in the share of the population unfamiliar with the circumstances surrounding the creation of the Permanent Fund and by the increase over time in the size of the dividend payment. Some supporters have suggested protecting the dividend payment, now at the discretion of the legislature, by putting it into the state constitution. For now it seems well protected simply by the strength of its popularity. But for every argument in support of the dividend, there is one opposed. The list includes the following:

—The dividend should be reinvested in the Permanent Fund to better provide for our future needs.

—We should be investing the dividend money in something tangible, like physical infrastructure, to help stimulate economic development.

—Much of the dividend is spent on frivolous consumption goods—alcohol and other items.

—Many people use their dividends to take vacations, thus spending their money out of state.

—A big chunk of dividend dollars must be paid to the federal government in higher personal taxes. We should spend the dividend money in ways that don't leak out of the state.

—We should not be giving money away if we want to convince the federal government to keep sending us grants based on need.

—The dividend fosters a culture of dependence on government that is neither healthy nor sustainable.

—The dividend fosters a culture of consumption, when what Alaska needs is more investment.

—The dividend attracts undesirable people to move into the state, putting a burden on current residents.

—There is no reason the government should be giving checks to Alaskan millionaires.

—The dividend makes it impossible to use any Permanent Fund earnings to finance essential government services.

—Life is great in Alaska. There is no need to pay me just to live here.

Between the supporters and opponents of the dividend are those who recognize its overwhelming popularity, but fear it will become too big, which has generally meant an amount slightly larger than the current dividend. But suggestions to cap the dividend at $500, $1,000 or some larger amount have never garnered much support.

Alaskans are in agreement that Alaska has the right to the resource rents from petroleum production on state land. They disagree on whether ownership rests with the people communally or individually. If communally, then decisions about how to spend the royalties from oil should be made by the legislature representing the citizens of the state. If individually, then the citizens as individuals should make those decisions.

Those who consider the ownership to be communal are more likely to view the dividend as a government program that distributes income. Those who consider the ownership to be individual are more likely to view the dividend as a distribution of their ownership share of the petroleum wealth and to view the government role as simply facilitating that distribution.

Because of these two viewpoints, some Alaskans, as well as many non-Alaskans, view the dividend as a socialistic government handout, while at the same time many other Alaskans view it as a payment based on a private property right. Those who view it as a government handout decry the entitlement mentality they see fostered by the payment. Those who view it as a property right feel the government has no business getting involved in managing its disposition.

These different viewpoints have existed since the dividend was introduced and show no sign of resolution.

Economic and Social Effects of the Petroleum Fund Dividend

One concern with a natural resource windfall is that when spent locally, it will overheat an economy and thus lead to inflation, erode competitiveness, and eventually slow economic growth. In a state within a nation, as Alaska is, this is less of a concern because its open border allows increases in local demand to be met by in-migration of goods, services, and workers, thus minimizing the inflationary pressure from increased spending.

The Permanent Fund acts as a buffer between the collection of petroleum revenues and the spending of those revenues. By removing the automatic connection between the two, it has a moderating effect on the economic boom created by the windfall—both in the present and in the future. It siphons part of the windfall away from current spending and reallocates it to some future time.

The current practice of the Permanent Fund is not the only way to moderate this connection. If all the fund's earnings to date had been reinvested, it would be worth twice as much today. Alaskans would be able to spend more in the future because they had spent less in the past. Another distribution scheme that was initially proposed was to put all petroleum revenues into a special fund from which the earnings would be drawn to spend on public programs. This would have ensured that the economy would not become overheated in the short term, though perhaps shifts benefits of the windfall too much toward future generations.[18]

Alaskans are most interested in how their friends and neighbors spend their dividend checks. The infusion of cash increases the demand for consumer goods and services that generate employment and payroll growth, particularly in the retail and service parts of the economy. The increase in purchasing power cascades through the financial system producing additional employment and payroll until it leaks out of the stream of local purchases as purchases outside the region, savings, and taxes. The newly created jobs would mostly be filled by workers from outside the state who will bring their families with them. According to one estimate, ultimately the economy will be larger by roughly 7,000 additional jobs and $1.1 billion (2010 $) in additional personal income; about 12,000 more people will move into the state.[19] A more precise estimate is impossible because little is known about exactly how households spend their dividends.

The economic and social effects of the dividend have not been studied much. Alaskans tend to view the disposition of dividend income as a private matter. Even if it were viewed as a public program rather than a distribution of earnings, there is little tradition in Alaska for program evaluation. Furthermore, because almost everyone in the state receives the dividend, it is difficult to construct statistical analyses that allow researchers to isolate the effects of the dividend from all the other factors simultaneously impacting behavior. And finally, much of the data that would go into such studies are not of high enough quality to support rigorous statistical analyses.

A popular method for determining what people have done with their dividend checks is to ask them directly when they have them in hand. An informal survey conducted by the Permanent Fund Corp. in 1994 reported that three-quarters of respondents planned to save half or more of their dividend (including reducing their level of debt).[20] Although this indicates what people did with their checks when they got them, it does not tell us how the dividend affects their consumption behavior. For example, some people said they used their dividend to buy winter clothes for their children. While it may be true that the dividend check was used in that way, it is unlikely that most parents, had they not received a dividend, would have deprived their children of winter coats in the harsh northern environment.

Alaskans have come to expect the dividend each year. Although they understand that its exact size will not be known until shortly before it is distributed, they tend to treat it as a permanent increase in their income. Consistent with the permanent income hypothesis, they will spread the additional consumption made possible by the dividend over their entire lifetime, probably on more of the same types of goods and services they would have consumed without the dividend income. According to this theory, consumption should not increase noticeably at the time of the dividend distribution.

However, the anecdotal evidence, responses of people when directly asked, and a study of the pattern of receipts at retail outlets in communities across the state suggest that consumer purchases, as distinct from consumption, do tend to concentrate around the time that the dividend checks arrive. One reason for this is that a large dividend or the combination of several dividends together provides some recipients with the "liquidity" necessary to buy an expensive consumer durable that provides consumption benefits lasting a long time—appliances, snow machines, and the like. Hence the concentration of these consumer-durable purchases is not inconsistent with the permanent income hypothesis of smoothed consumption.

A second reason for purchases concentrated during the dividend distribution season is that businesses compete for a share of the dividend dollars through advertising campaigns, sales, and other types of special offers. Timing the purchase of a new boat motor or a trip to Hawaii with the dividend distribution season can be a smart consumer decision. It also is a happy coincidence for retailers that the distribution comes at the beginning of the Christmas shopping season when people are in a mood to spend.[21]

Even though spending increases when the dividend is distributed, anecdotal evidence suggests that a large share of the distribution is saved. This was to be expected in the early years of the program since people did not know if it would continue and thus viewed it as a windfall. Although that is no longer the case, the fact that the dividend is a large lump sum might provide an incentive for some saving that would not otherwise occur. The savings by parents of dividends paid to children is more likely even more significant.

looking for the dividend's lasting impacts, one finds that no entity has tried to demonstrate that the additional discretionary income, either spent or saved, has enhanced the economic well-being of Alaskan households. Nor has anyone tried to demonstrate that the dividend has expanded economic development activities. Some fear that the dividend has created a consumption-oriented environment and that households have not used the opportunity it provides to increase their private wealth or to increase their personal freedom.

But this begs the question of how the success of the program should be evaluated. Without the dividend program, the money would most likely have been spent on activities designed to strengthen and diversify the economy—physical infrastructure, loan programs for businesses and households, and expenditures to support development of new industrial activities. But the state has spent a considerable amount on these activities with only limited success. Much of this spending that targets economic development could better be characterized as consumption rather than investment in that it has produced temporary economic growth, but not necessarily sustained development.

Furthermore, strictly on the basis of income delivered to Alaska households—an important criterion for public expenditures in Alaska— the dividend does a better job than capital investments or government spending on operations.[22]

Two of the dividend's features allow it to help level the income distribution: it is distributed equally to all residents, and the federal government considers it taxable as personal income. The dividend adds a larger percentage to after-tax income at the lower end of the distribution than at the upper end.[23]

The dividend establishes a floor below which the cash income of residents cannot fall, but it is not large enough by itself to provide a basic level of income for a household and was never designed for that purpose. There are a number of federal and state safety net programs like Social Security, the earned income tax credit, unemployment insurance, and food stamps that help lift people above the poverty level, which, according to guidelines set by the U.S. Department of Health and Human Services, is $18,210 for a two-person household in Alaska.[24] Consequently as an addition to these safety nets, the dividend has been one factor in the decline in the official poverty rate since Alaska attained statehood, particularly among Native Alaskans. The Native Alaskan poverty rate fell from 25 percent to 19 percent between the census years of 1980 and 1990.[25]

The dividend is particularly important in rural parts of the state where the economy is largely a mixture of government cash-based transfers and subsistence activities, and where cash employment is scarce. Households are cash-poor, and the subsistence harvests can fluctuate dramatically from year to year. Under these circumstances the cash provided by the dividend is particularly important not only because of its size but also its relative predictability.

Although there is considerable migration out of these villages to locations with greater employment opportunities and better social services, most continue to exist because the residents prefer the subsistence lifestyle. Providing adequate public services to these communities is very expensive, and the social conditions are often poor. Although the dividend provides much needed cash to residents, it may be enabling or empowering people to remain in rural Alaska instead of moving to places where jobs are more readily available and public services less expensive. While it is difficult to weigh and compare the supportive and enabling effects of the dividend for residents of these communities, both effects need to be recognized.

Economic theory suggests that an unconditional payment like the dividend would reduce the supply of labor and increase the wage rate. In the University of Alaska's study of the early dividend program, only 1 percent of survey respondents reported they worked less because of the dividend. This is to be expected since many lower-income Alaskans, those most sensitive to an unconditional increase of income, would prefer more work but are constrained in their opportunity to obtain employment in the cash economy. On the other hand, the effects of a continuing dividend payment on labor supply might only become evident over time if workers choose to retire earlier.

No studies so far have tried to link the dividend to aspects of health or education status or other aspects of social well-being (like the crime rate). This is partly because Alaskans do not think of the dividend as a policy tool to address these problems and also because of the difficulty of identifying the effect of the dividend independent of other social welfare programs and influences. For the same reasons, no one has investigated the influence of the dividend on personal attitudes about empowerment, feelings of self-worth, sense of community, volunteerism, or other psychological factors.

One of the potential effects of the dividend that concerns many Alaskans is its impact on population. The dividend is a subsidy to the cost of raising a child, and that should increase the birth rate. In fact, an unpublished study has suggested the birth rate in Alaska has increased 18 percent because of the dividend.[26]

This seems unlikely for a number of reasons. First, there is no indication of such a large effect in a simple comparison of the trend in the Alaska birth rate with the rest of nation. Second, studies of direct child subsidies in other countries specifically designed to stimulate the birth rate fail to report such dramatic impacts. And third, the effect of the dividend program on the birth rate is complicated because while it does directly lower the cost of raising a child, it also increases household income. If the desired number of children falls with increasing income, the birth rate could potentially go down as a result of introduction of the dividend program.

It is more likely that the dividend would influence population because it acts as a "population magnet." The dividend is an obvious incentive to move to Alaska, independent of any increase in employment opportunities arising from jobs created by residents spending their dividends. This effect should be concentrated among lower-income people and anyone not closely connected to the labor market.[27] This population growth dilutes the size of the dividend and puts increased demand on public services.

The over-sixty-five population is increasing at a rate faster than in any other state, and demand for public as well as for nonprofit programs providing services for lower-income individuals and families has also been growing rapidly. But it is difficult to sort out the causes for these increases among various public programs and to be able to attribute any of it to the dividend. No one responding to the 1984 survey indicated that he or she had moved to Alaska to get the dividend, and almost no respondents said they had decided not to move out of the state because of the dividend.

But the dividend could also attract people who are in the labor market. Relative wages in a region reflect differences in the cost of living and private and public amenities. The high wage in Alaska is compensation for the high cost of living, the rough climate, and absence of many private amenities. The introduction of a dividend increases the attractiveness of Alaska and should be reflected in a compensating reduction in the wage rate as the labor supply increases when more people are attracted to the state.[28]

If that were to occur, part of the dividend's benefit would go to those businesses able to hire low-wage workers. The possibility of this type of effect underscores the necessity of considering what economists call the "general equilibrium" effects of cash transfers. When a policy like the dividend program is large enough to cause changes in relative prices that influence the allocation of resources and behavior, then looking only at direct effects will not capture all the important effects of that policy and could lead to incorrect conclusions about its benefits.

The dividend has clearly shifted a considerable amount of resource wealth spending from the public to the private sector. But fiscal discipline should be defined more narrowly than that, to mean measuring the benefits of public expenditures against the private loss from paying for them. Dividend supporters argue that the dividend substitutes for the missing personal income tax as the means of imposing fiscal discipline on the state budget. In theory, the dividend needs to compete each year against other uses of fund earnings. But in practice that discipline is imposed only when other revenues are insufficient to completely fund the state budget. It is only then that the trade-off between funding the dividend or using the money to pay for public services is clearly delineated. At other times additional means must be relied upon to impose discipline on the budget-making process.

Consequently one can argue that the public budgeting process would be more balanced if a special account were in place dedicated only to paying the annual dividend. Therefore deliberations and decisions regarding the regular operating and capital budgets did not have to take into account their impact on the size of the dividend.

The dividend is part of a unique fiscal system that results in an unusual relationship between the government and the people. An entire generation of Alaskans has been raised having received a dividend annually since birth without necessarily understanding the purpose for which it was created. This generation has also never experienced paying for the state services they have received because petroleum revenues have covered all costs. This has fostered a distorted idea of the true cost of government and the sense that the role of the state is to provide public services at no cost and also to hand out cash to all citizens.

For some citizens, this means that their only connection with the state government is the Permanent Fund dividend check they receive. Furthermore, because there are no personal taxes and receipt of the dividend carries no public responsibilities, the two together undermine the sense of community that comes from the need to collectively choose and fund public services. An alternative to the current dividend program would be a community dividend distributed to each community based on the number of residents. Residents would be free to spend the community dividend any way they wanted, but they would have to jointly determine how it would be used. This would build community involvement. Under such an arrangement, it might be more likely that the money would purchase physical facilities that would produce continuing benefits for residents—current and future. This would keep more of the money in Alaska (it would not be subject to the income tax or residents leaving with their dividend) and at the same time increase the incentive for community action. Of course, the community dividend could also be used to reduce the local tax burden.

Declining Petroleum Production and the Challenge Ahead

The Permanent Fund and the dividend face their biggest challenge in the coming decades.

Alaska has relied almost entirely on petroleum revenues to fund government (about 89 percent) for nearly forty years. But in the last twenty years production has dropped by two-thirds and is projected to continue to decline at the same rate. In recent years the high price of oil has swelled the state treasury, but eventually petroleum revenues will fall with the inevitable decline in production. Growth of the Permanent Fund will slow as the deposit of royalty revenue slows. The high petroleum revenues have contributed to growth of the economy, but the development of an alternative tax base to replace petroleum has not followed.

There are two revenue sources available to replace declining petroleum revenues. The first is taxing households.[29] Alaska is the only state with neither a personal income tax nor a general sales tax. The second is the income of the Permanent Fund. Taken together, they would generate considerably less revenue than petroleum, so many people think both of these alternative revenue sources would be needed in the future to pay for public services.

The Permanent Fund was created to ensure that future generations of Alaskans would share in the benefits from the petroleum wealth. Shortly thereafter, the Permanent Fund dividend was created to ensure that the benefits to the current generation would be equitable and that there would be a constituency to protect the fund from attack. This constituency would serve as a proxy for those future generations not represented in the decisionmaking process.

Some would argue that this constituency has taken over the fund and turned it, de facto, into one that exists for the sole purpose of paying the Permanent Fund dividend. It has been converted from a savings account into an income distribution fund. This is evident from the fact that many people now mistakenly refer to the Alaska Permanent Fund as the Alaska Permanent Dividend Fund.[30]

The current practice regarding the distribution of fund income is first to pay the dividend, then to inflation-proof the fund, and finally to leave any remainder in the contingency account; doing so covers potential future income shortfalls that would otherwise make it impossible to fully fund the dividend and inflation-proof the fund. Although the remainder fluctuates from year to year, it has averaged several hundred million dollars, and the balance in the contingency account tends to grow over time.

There have been several attempts in the past, during periods of low petroleum revenues, to use the funds in this contingency account to help pay the costs of government operations. In the late 1980s a suggestion known as the 40-30-30 rule would have allocated 40 percent of income to the dividend, 30 percent to inflation proofing, and 30 percent to general fund spending through a new budget reserve fund. It was proposed as an equitable distribution of earnings among current residents, future generations (inflation proofing), and public needs. The rule was not adopted.

An advisory vote in 1999 that asked if Permanent Fund income left after paying the dividend and inflation proofing should be used to help balance the state budget was defeated with 83 percent opposed. The fact that the governor called for an advisory vote on this question is particularly significant because the legislature already had the authority to appropriate not only the funds in the contingency account, but also all the fund's earnings.

This example demonstrates how sensitive policymakers have become to the suggestion to use fund earnings for financing state government expenditures. Most are loath to entertain such a suggestion for fear of being charged with mounting an attack against the dividend. It has even been suggested that the only way to resolve the impasse is to cash out the entire Permanent Fund in one large distribution so the public would no longer obsess over it.

However, there is an opposing point of view that the dividend is not an impediment to a solution to the long-term fiscal problem faced by the state. This view, espoused by late Governor Jay Hammond, is that the best way to balance public against private consumption is not to give the legislature direct access to the earnings of the Permanent Fund. Instead, give all the fund's income to residents and require that the government "claw back"—in the form of income or other taxes—whatever it can convince the public is necessary to pay for public services.

When petroleum revenues have disappeared, financing government through an income tax rather than fund earnings would have several advantages. First, it imposes a direct link between the cost of public services and their perceived benefits. Second, the incidence of the burden of paying for government with an income tax would be progressive whereas reducing the dividend would be regressive. Third, cutting the dividend would put the burden entirely on residents whereas nonresidents would pay a share of an income tax. And finally, because a state income tax is deductible from the federal income tax, the federal government would be paying a portion of the cost of state government.

Arguments that support reducing the dividend rather than imposing an income tax include the apparent inefficiency of the government handing out money with one hand (the dividend) and taking it back with the other through taxation, the inequity of putting the burden of paying for government only on workers, and the disincentive to work and invest created by an income tax.

In the end, given the high cost of government in Alaska, even imposing an income tax at rates considered confiscatory would probably not generate enough revenue to cover the cost of a very basic level of government services. So some change in the way fund income is distributed will become necessary.

A third possible outcome for the problem of funding state government in the future would be to use the Permanent Fund itself to balance the budget. This could be done without contravening the language of the constitutional amendment prohibiting expenditure of the fund itself in either of two ways. The state could borrow against the balance to finance government, or it could stop inflation proofing. Either would reduce the real value of fund assets over time, so this alternative is not an attractive outcome.

As petroleum revenues fall, this debate will intensify. As the state moves into a post-petroleum future, it is fortunate to have the Permanent Fund as a resource to help it make that transition. Whether that transition will be successful remains to be determined.

Notes

1. Royalties have accounted for 49 percent of total petroleum revenues. Of the state taxes collected on petroleum activity—production, income, and property—the production tax is the most important, having accounted for 37 percent of total petroleum revenues. Petroleum income taxes have accounted for 10 percent.

2. This was in the form of a temporary reserves tax that was credited against future production taxes.

3. The Alaska Constitution prohibits dedicated funds, so an amendment was required to establish the Alaska Permanent Fund.

4. Contributions from fields leased after 1979 are 50 percent of royalties. Yet these fields have been small relative to the early discoveries.

5. The deposits from these sources are constitutionally protected from being spent and are called the "fund corpus." The market value of the fund at any time will be greater or less than this, due to unrealized gains or losses on investments.

6. The amount of the annual inflation-proofing deposit is equal to the value of cumulative deposits at the end of the previous year multiplied by the percent change in the consumer price index over the current year. This deposit is paid out of the realized earnings of the fund as an annual legislative appropriation.

7. Neither the dividend nor the inflation-proofing formula depends on current year fund income.

8. Alaska Permanent Fund Corp., *2007 Annual Financial Report*, p. 26.

9. Under the Percent of Market Value (POMV) proposal, the fund would establish a target real rate of return and each year draw no more than that percent from the fund as income. Implementation of this proposal would require passing a constitutional referendum.

10. See Peter J. Smith, "The Politics of Plenty: Investing Natural Resource Revenues in Alberta and Alaska," *Canadian Public Policy* 17 (June 1991), pp. 139–54.

11. See www.apfc.org/home.

12. Interestingly, the state already had a cash distribution program when the dividend was proposed. The Longevity Bonus Program, created shortly after statehood, provided monthly cash payment of $100 to each person older than sixty-five who had lived in Alaska for at least twenty-five years and was a resident at the time of statehood. The program was later expanded to include everyone older than sixty-five regardless of length of residence; it has since been phased out.

13. Because the dividend formula is based on the five-year moving average of fund income, it is possible that current-year income could be insufficient to fully fund a dividend payment. So the fund maintains a contingency account that covers any shortfall in current-year income. This account is known as the earnings reserve.

14. The first dividend of $1,000 was not paid out of Permanent Fund earnings.

15. Since personal income, as defined by the U.S. Department of Commerce's Bureau of Economic Analysis, includes nonwage earnings (benefits) and government medical payments not directly received by households, this probably somewhat underestimates the importance of the dividend as a share of income as perceived by many households.

16. Gunnar Knapp and others, "The Alaska Permanent Fund Dividend Program: Economic Effects and Public Attitudes," Institute of Social and Economic Research, University of Alaska Anchorage, 1984.

17. Alaska Permanent Fund Corp., Trustee Papers, 1989, p. 63.

18. This suggestion was advocated by the Alaska attorney Roger Cremo and was known as the Cremo Plan. The Norwegian fund has adopted a version of this approach.

19. Because the size of the dividend fluctuates, this estimate represents an average over time. For a detailed analysis, see Scott Goldsmith and Jeff Wanamaker, "The Economic Impact of the Alaska Permanent Fund Dividend," Institute of Social and Economic Research, University of Alaska Anchorage, 1989.

20. See Gordon Harrison, "The Economics and Politics of the Alaska Permanent Fund Dividend Program," in *Alaska Public Policy Issues*, ed. Clive Thomas (Juneau: Denali Press, 1999), pp. 81–91.

21. One study of the dividend concluded that consumption did not change at the time of the distribution. See Chang-Tai Hsieh, "Do Consumers React to Anticipated Income Changes? Evidence from the Alaska Permanent Fund," *American Economic Review* 93 (March 2003), pp. 397–405.

22. Scott Goldsmith, "A Comparative Analysis of the Economic Effects of Reimposing Personal Income Taxes, Reducing Permanent Fund Dividends, or Reducing State Spending," report, Institute of Social and Economic Research, University of Alaska Anchorage, 1987.

23. Between the early 1980s and the early 2000s, the after-tax income of the richest 20 percent of families increased at a faster rate than that of the poorest 20 percent in thirty-eight states. In the twenty-two other states, growth rates were about the same for the two groups. Alaska was the only state in which the income of the bottom 20 percent grew at a faster rate (25 percent) than the income of the top 20 percent (10 percent). In the early 1980s Alaska had the greatest income inequality of any state, measured by the ratio of average income of the top 20 percent of families compared with the lowest 20 percent—six to six. By the early 2000s Alaska had fallen to forty-third place at five to eight, while the U.S. average had increased from five to five to

seven to three. The trend toward greater income equality in Alaska was due both to faster growth in incomes of families at the bottom of the distribution—25 percent compared with 19 percent for the total United States—and to slower growth in incomes of families at the top of the distribution—10 percent compared with 59 percent for the country. See Jared Bernstein and others, *Pulling Apart: A State-by-State Analysis of Income Trends* (Washington, D.C.: Center for Budget and Policy Priorities and Economic Policy Institute, 2006).

24. These guidelines set in 2009 are used in the determination of eligibility for many, but not all, federal assistance programs. The guidelines are higher for Alaska than other states because of the high cost of living, but they do not reflect differences in the cost of living across regions within the state.

25. Scott Goldsmith and others, *The Status of Alaska Natives Report,* prepared for the Alaska Federation of Natives, Institute of Social and Economic Research, University of Alaska Anchorage, 2004. The census poverty rate is based on the poverty threshold, a definition that varies with household composition but does not account for the higher cost of living in Alaska relative to other states. Because the relative cost of living has fallen in Alaska since statehood, one would expect the calculated poverty rate to increase if all other variables were constant. Thus the reported decline in the poverty rate over time is an underestimate of the actual trend in the population's well-being.

26. See Yereth Rosen, "In Alaska, a Push to Curb Perks for Citizens," *Christian Science Monitor,* May 10, 2006.

27. The case of "Papa Pilgrim" garnered considerable media attention early in the decade spanning 2000–10 after it was reported that he had moved to Alaska and settled in a remote location with his wife and fifteen children. It seemed clear to most Alaskans that his primary motive was to collect the dividend check and live off the land and state government services.

28. One reviewer suggested that this effect could be offset if the dividend led to an increase in the bargaining power of workers relative to employers.

29. Nonhousehold taxes could not generate much revenue for several reasons. First, only a small share of Alaska businesses are organized as corporations, so most are not liable for the corporate income tax. A personal income tax would capture a share of the business profits of noncorporate businesses. Second, much of the state's economic base is based on federal government activities that are not taxable. Finally, the nonwage gross product of the other resource industries—mining, seafood, and timber—is very small.

30. The more the Permanent Fund comes to look like a trust fund for individuals, the more likely it is that the federal government would attempt to tax the fund income.

4

Saving Iraq from Its Oil

NANCY BIRDSALL and ARVIND SUBRAMANIAN

Escaping the Resource Curse

As the United States, the United Nations, and the Iraqi Governing Council struggle to determine what form Iraq's next government should take, one question more than any other may prove critical to the country's future: how to handle its vast oil wealth. Oil riches are far from the blessing they are often assumed to be. In fact, countries often end up poor precisely because they are oil rich. Oil and mineral wealth can be bad for growth and bad for democracy, since they tend to impede the development of institutions and values critical to open, market-based economies and political freedom: civil liberties, the rule of law, protection of property rights, and political participation. Plenty of examples illustrate what has come to be known as the "resource curse." Thanks to improvements in exploration technology, thirty-four less-developed countries now boast significant oil and natural gas resources that constitute at least 30 percent of their total export revenue (see box).

Despite their riches, however, twelve of these countries' annual per capita income remains below $1,500, and up to half of their population lives on less than $1 a day. Moreover, two-thirds of the thirty-four countries are not democratic, and of those that are, only three (Ecuador, São Tomé and Principe, and Trinidad and Tobago) score in the top half of Freedom House's world ranking of political freedom. And even these three states are fragile: Ecuador now teeters on the brink of renewed

Less-Developed Countries with Major Oil and Natural Gas Resources		
Algeria	Equatorial Guinea	Russia
Angola	Gabon	São Tomé and Principe
Azerbaijan	Iran	Saudi Arabia
Bahrain	Iraq	Sudan
Brunei	Kazakhstan	Syria
Cameroon	Kuwait	Trinidad and Tobago
Chad	Kyrgyz Republic	Tunisia
Colombia	Libya	Turkmenistan
Democratic Republic of the	Mexico	United Arab Emirates
Congo	Nigeria	Venezuela
Ecuador	Oman	Yemen
Egypt	Qatar	

instability, and in São Tomé and Principe, the temptations created by sudden oil wealth are straining its democracy and its relations with next-door Nigeria.

In fact, the thirty-four oil-rich countries share one striking similarity: they have weak, or in some cases nonexistent, political and economic institutions. This problem may not seem surprising for the several African countries on the list, such as Angola and the Democratic Republic of the Congo, that have only recently emerged from civil conflict. But it is also a problem for the newly independent, oil- and gas-rich republics of the former Soviet Union, which have done little to consolidate property and contract rights or to ensure competent management or judicial independence. And even the richer countries on the list, such as Libya and Saudi Arabia, suffer from underdeveloped political institutions. Concentrated oil wealth at the top has forestalled political change.

Can Iraq avoid the pitfalls that other oil-rich countries have fallen into? The answer is yes, but only if it is willing to implement a novel arrangement for managing its oil wealth with the help of the international community. This arrangement should not mimic the much-maligned oil-for-food program set up in the aftermath of the Persian Gulf War, under which Iraq's oil income was directly controlled and administered by foreigners. Instead, the Iraqi people should embed in their new constitution an arrangement for the direct distribution of oil revenues to all Iraqi households—an arrangement that would be supervised by the international community.

From Manna to Witches' Brew

To understand the corrupting effect that oil can have on a country, it is useful to understand the way thinking about development has changed over the last five decades. Development theory—the prevailing view of how to ensure economic and political development in nonindustrialized countries—has evolved through three phases. In the first phase, in vogue until the 1970s, development experts emphasized augmenting a society's physical capital or "hardware," such as its dams, roads, and power plants. Following the popular success of the Marshall Plan in Europe and what was then seen as the success of the Soviet model, the World Bank, the United States, and other official donors concentrated on financing infrastructure-related projects in the world's poor countries. The approach promised to deliver quick and visible results for newly independent governments shaking off the yoke of colonial rule.

In the second phase, popular during the 1980s, the ideological pendulum shifted to getting poor countries to pursue liberal economic policies—including opening themselves up to trade and foreign investment, reducing the role of the state, encouraging competition through privatization and deregulation, and maintaining sound fiscal policy. This approach, later dubbed the "Washington consensus," was driven by disenchantment with the meager results of the hardware approach and a widespread recognition that appropriate economic incentives were necessary to stimulate private sector participation in an economy.

In the 1990s, the development community gave up on the expectation that growth would automatically trickle down and turned to health, education, and other investments to reduce poverty directly. By the end of the 1990s, however, it had become clear that even the right hardware, the right policies, and the right poverty-focused programs would not guarantee sustained growth and development. Latin America, for example—a champion of privatization and openness to trade—managed a growth rate of only 1.6 percent per capita during the 1990s despite major increases in infrastructure and social spending, whereas growth in sub-Saharan Africa declined by 0.2 percent a year despite massive externally funded investments and the constant guidance of the World Bank and the International Monetary Fund. Meanwhile, the economies of eastern Asia, especially China's, grew rapidly during this period, despite their obvious deviations from the liberal model.

The prevailing view of development theory has thus started to shift again. Today, experts emphasize the "software" of an economy: the institutions, customs, laws, and social cohesion that help to create and sustain markets. Good software can come in many forms, ranging from the European Union's independent central bank to the ingenious Chinese experiment with the village enterprise system. In some societies, software can take less tangible forms: the long-standing trust that exists between private contracting Chinese parties, for example, was key to the investments from expatriate Chinese that fueled early growth in Malaysia and now in China. In other places, it takes the form of enforceable property titles and contracts and an uncorrupted court system.

Conversely, it is becoming increasingly clear that economies without the right software will falter. Poor supervision of banks can lead to financial crises; civil service systems without performance standards and rewards undermine public services; and abuses of property rights discourage small business.

The problem for newly reconstituted states such as Iraq is that growth-friendly institutions cannot simply be imported. They must be nurtured domestically over long periods of time. And time is a luxury that troubled developing countries with vast natural wealth rarely have.

Throughout history, many countries with natural resources have fared worse than "poorer" nations. In the seventeenth century, the Netherlands outdid resource-rich Spain, despite the fact that the latter's coffers were overflowing with gold and silver acquired in the New World. Similarly, Japan and Switzerland moved past Russia in the nineteenth and twentieth centuries. More recently, resource-poor countries in eastern Asia have surged ahead of resource-rich Argentina, Mexico, Nigeria, and Venezuela, all of which repeatedly went bankrupt or lapsed into political upheaval. Natural resources may seem like manna from heaven at first, providing new states the means to escape poverty and invest in schools and roads. And indeed, sometimes the money is spent wisely, as in Kuwait and Bahrain. More often, however, such riches prove a curse.

There are several explanations for why oil undermines societies. World prices for oil and similar resources are notoriously volatile, especially compared to those for manufactured goods, and so countries that rely on the export of natural resources are exposed to much greater uncertainty and risk. Fluctuations in price can create a dangerous cycle in which governments spend wildly when they are flush, only to be forced into disruptive and costly spending cuts (leaving schools without teachers or public buildings unfinished) when prices fall.

A second explanation for the oil curse is the so-called Dutch disease. As the Netherlands experienced when it discovered natural gas in the North Sea in the 1960s, the exploitation of mineral resources can crowd out other activities in a country's economy. When resources are discovered or their prices increase, a country's currency becomes stronger. This hurts domestic manufacturers, who soon find it difficult to compete with lower-priced imports. More of the country's labor and capital starts to be deployed in local nontradeable sectors, and unless corrective steps are taken, soon the whole country suffers, since it loses the benefits—such as technological innovation and good management—that a strong domestic manufacturing sector can provide.

The most important explanation for the oil curse, however, has to do with the role natural resources play in impeding the development of a society's economic and political institutions. Oil works its poison in many ways. Natural resources, unlike output created by human endeavor, yield large "rents," which are rewards in excess of effort. But such rents are easy to appropriate—either by the state or by the few who control the resources' extraction. In the former case, as in Iran, Libya, and Saudi Arabia, one set of problems arises. The state is relieved of the pressure to tax and has no incentive to promote the protection of property rights as a way of creating wealth. As for the country's citizens, because they are not taxed, they have little incentive and no effective mechanism by which to hold government accountable. This can lead to the unchecked abuse of state power and undermine the process by which political systems reconcile conflicting interests and demands. Indeed, such conditions make it very hard for political institutions to develop.

When a subset of the population is able to control the natural resource wealth, meanwhile, it can "buy" or "become" the state, as occurred in Angola or in what was then Zaire (now the Democratic Republic of the Congo). Even where the state and those who control its resources remain distinct (as in Russia and Venezuela), public officials tend to become corrupt. Vicious fights over the distribution of resources often result. These battles are often portrayed as ethnic rivalries, when in fact they may actually be simply fights to monopolize wealth. Even when the resulting problems do not explode into outright civil conflicts, they discourage investment and growth and corrode political institutions.

According to economic historians, this pattern explains the very different ways North and South America developed. In the latter, large plantations of sugar allowed landed elites to maintain concentrated economic and political control, and these elites resisted democratic reforms and the institution of property rights. In North America, by contrast, the cultivation of wheat and corn on small farms led to a dispersion of economic power and more favorable conditions for democratization and institutional development.

Scarce Success

Nowhere have all the pathologies associated with oil manifested themselves more clearly than in Nigeria. In the late 1960s, the Biafran war of secession—then Africa's biggest civil war, which killed a million people—was, in part, an attempt by the country's eastern, predominantly Igbo, region to gain exclusive control over oil reserves. Nigeria has also suffered the assassination of two of its leaders, six successful coups and four failed ones, and thirty years of military rule. Its "pirates in power," as one Africa historian called its leaders, have plundered Nigeria's oil wealth to the tune of perhaps $100 billion. The explosion in windfall-financed government expenditures has also provided increased opportunities for kickbacks. All of these forces have contributed to poor economic growth and other staggeringly malign results. Between 1970 and 2000, the number of people living below the poverty line in Nigeria increased from 19 million to nearly 90 million, and inequality widened: the top 2 percent of the population, which earned as much as the bottom 17 percent in 1970, now earns as much as the bottom 55 percent. Nor are such statistics unique to Nigeria. In different forms and at different times, natural-resource wealth has wreaked similar havoc in Angola, Equatorial Guinea, Gabon, and Venezuela, and now threatens to affect tiny São Tomé and Principe. In Angola, an estimated $4.2 billion has gone missing from government coffers over the last few years. In Venezuela, poverty has nearly doubled since the late 1970s and the share of national income going to business owners has increased from 50 percent to nearly 80 percent; as a result, ordinary workers now get a mere 20 percent of the economic pie.

The oil-rich countries of the Middle East have so far escaped some of the worst side effects of mineral wealth—but only because of the sheer magnitude of their oil resources relative to the size of their populations. And they have not avoided the stunted political and social development associated with oil. The UN Development Program's 2002 *Human Development Report* identified the lack of press and other freedoms and the low status of women as key obstacles to the Arab world's long-run progress. Moreover, although current economic performance in the Middle East may be broadly satisfactory, it cannot be expected to remain so for long. Venezuela shows how even a relatively affluent country can deteriorate over time as the fight over easy oil wealth corrodes its political and economic institutions.

Indeed, amid all the examples of countries undermined by their own resource riches, two success stories stand out: Norway and Botswana. And even these examples serve only to reinforce the dangerous impact of natural resources. Norway discovered its oil in the 1970s, well after it had developed mechanisms for accountability. The country survived its sudden boom because well-entrenched checks and balances prevented oil revenues from being wasted or siphoned off. Decisions about how to spend oil money were taken through the normal democratic process.

Even more interesting is the case of Botswana, which has mined diamonds for several decades. Botswana did not succumb to the resource curse because it is one of the few countries in Africa that emerged from British rule in 1966 with strong institutions, thanks to pre-existing local and tribal traditions that fostered broad political participation. Fortunately, colonial administration never penetrated deeply enough into Botswana to destroy these traditions, which, after independence, formed the foundation for a functioning democracy. Uninterrupted democracy and good political leadership have ensured that the rents from natural resources were not squandered, as they have been elsewhere in Africa.

Norway and Botswana illustrate that the natural resource curse can be avoided if states have institutions strong enough to cushion themselves from the usual malign influences. Oil and other natural resources do not predestine all developing countries to failure. Indonesia and Mexico provide guarded optimism that the oil curse can be avoided. Although Indonesia has suffered economic and political setbacks ever since the onset of the Asian financial crisis in 1997, it did enjoy two decades of sustained growth and poverty reduction before the crisis hit. Meanwhile, Mexico has also managed its oil responsibly, and in 2000 elected an opposition candidate, Vicente Fox, as president. In both cases, however, the jury is still out on whether they will be able to durably defy the oil curse. Chile and Malaysia provide even better examples. Although they started the development race economically poor, institutionally weak, and heavily dependent on resources (copper in Chile and rubber in Malaysia), they have subsequently managed to grow rapidly and escape resource dependence.

Cure for the Curse

Given how bad oil and other natural resources have proved for the development of markets and political freedom, how should they be managed in Iraq and other countries? Three options should be considered: privatizing oil resources, creating special oil funds that limit government discretion in spending the money, and transferring the proceeds from oil directly to the people. The first approach—privatizing the oil sector—has proved disappointing. In countries with weak institutions, assets of immense value have too often been sold at throwaway prices to a lucky few who happen to have good financial or political connections. In Russia, for example, privatization of the country's Soviet oil companies and other resources only entrenched the economic imbalances of the status quo. The resulting oligarchic capitalism has undermined Russia's market economy, making it more difficult to foster public trust in market institutions such as private property, the rule of law, and the sanctity of contracts. When privatization leads to greater economic imbalances, these in turn impede a country's transition to democracy or result, as in the case of Nigeria or Russia, in what *Newsweek*'s Fareed Zakaria has called "illiberal democracies." In such cases, elections are held periodically, but civil liberties are limited and the state sometimes undermines, rather than protects, individual freedom and property rights. Oil tends to perpetuate the power imbalances by favoring incumbents (who have easy access to oil resources) and encouraging patronage and corruption.

The second alternative for dealing with a country's oil wealth—the creation of special oil funds with constitutional or other restrictions on the use of revenues—has been used in Kuwait and Norway for several decades, and in Colombia and Venezuela since the 1990s. Azerbaijan and Chad have also recently created such funds, and East Timor and São Tomé and Principe plan to do so this year. Although they vary in detail, these national oil funds all represent an attempt to insulate and render transparent the spending of some or all of a country's oil revenues. The funds are meant to help stabilize a country's spending— building up resources during the fat years to help the country weather lean ones—and to help it save revenues for the benefit of future generations. The newer funds also aim to force suddenly cash-rich governments to focus their spending on socially productive investments.

Unfortunately, apart from Norway (with its strong government institutions and healthy democracy), the experience of national oil funds has not been encouraging. In Venezuela, for example, the government has changed the rules stipulating how money in the oil fund should be spent six times in the last few years. As a result, the fund's resources have practically dried up, and it has not managed to ensure prudent revenue management or an improvement in the quality of spending. In Azerbaijan, ad hoc expenditures from the fund have also started to raise questions about its long-term promise. And in Chad, where the oil fund was created as a condition of a World Bank loan to help finance an oil pipeline, the country's president—despite oversight by nongovernmental organizations—still managed to use the first wave of revenue to buy a presidential airplane. Although the fund itself was not actually raided, the airplane purchase was unexpected and inconsistent with the overall budget program agreed on by Chad and its international creditors. Oil funds, therefore, seem unable to insulate oil revenues from appropriation by weak or unaccountable governments. They are no substitutes for public accountability or for the checks and balances provided by the press and a healthy democracy.

The third alternative for managing a country's oil wealth—distributing it directly to the people—has a better record, at least in the few places (the state of Alaska and the Canadian province of Alberta) where it has been tried. (In both cases, the interest from oil funds, rather than oil revenue itself, is distributed.) Such systems minimize opportunities for corruption and misappropriation, since windfall revenue stays out of the hands of public officials. They also avoid the imbalance of economic and political power associated with private control of revenues. Moreover, in developing countries, the direct distribution of oil revenues would instantly increase per capita income, sometimes substantially. In Chad, for example, where per capita income is about $200 a year, equally distributing the country's expected net oil revenues among its population would increase average income by 20 percent in 2008; in São Tomé and Principe, the increase would be greater still. Such an increase would enable parents to keep their children in school, help farm producers diversify, and stimulate more government investment in roads and other infrastructure. In other words, distribution of oil revenues would aid the development of homegrown markets and local politics.

Proposals to distribute oil revenues to the public, however, are often met with two standard objections: that the loss of oil revenue to the government could cause macroeconomic instability, and that distributing revenues to the people only to then partially tax them back to finance public investment and other sensible government expenditures is inefficient. Neither objection is compelling. In macroeconomic terms, channeling oil wealth to the public instead of government shifts the problem of price volatility to individual households. And in countries with weak institutions, households are much better at managing volatility than is the government; in fact, they are better judges not only of how much to spend, but of what to spend it on. Recent history is replete with examples of governments creating white elephants during revenue upsurges, such as Indonesia's benighted commercial jet industry or Nigeria's infamous Ajakouta steel complex (which has not produced a single ton of saleable steel in more than four decades). It is hard to imagine individual investors making mistakes of such magnitude or duration.

The second objection—that distribution followed by taxation is wasteful—has some logic. But the costs in efficiency are eclipsed by the benefits of encouraging public scrutiny of government spending. Governments that derive revenues from natural resources such as oil live in a dangerous supply-sider's paradise. When the marginal cost of raising public resources is virtually zero, governments have little incentive to manage well, provide adequate public services, respond to citizens' demands, or invest in and sustain the software of market economies and good governments. Ironically, good government and strong institutions require that the raising of public resources be costly.

Distributing oil revenues directly to people would be difficult in poor countries with limited administrative capacity, but not necessarily impossible. Before political problems overwhelmed Bolivia's reforms, for example, its government managed to distribute the "pension" returns from its share in privatized enterprises to all senior citizens. And although initially identifying all potential recipients and ensuring consistent and efficient distribution (probably via coupon-like vouchers) would be challenging, it would not be qualitatively different from that of immunizing children, which many poor countries have managed. It could in fact be easier, since citizens, eager for their windfall, would be quick to cooperate.

The greater problem with implementing a distribution plan would be political. Change would meet resistance on the part of current beneficiaries with a vested interest in the status quo, be they workers in a state-owned enterprise, oligarchs, or political incumbents. After the first year or so, moreover, the administrative apparatus for distribution would become vulnerable to cheating and corruption. Even immunization programs in poorer countries, for example, tend to need donor attention if they are to maintain their integrity.

Help from Outside

Luckily, Iraq is not as poor as Angola or Nigeria. And despite its current difficulties, Iraq is, in one respect, an economic policy practitioner's dream: it provides a relatively clean slate, allowing new policy approaches to be attempted with a minimum of resistance from vested interests. With the right solution in place—the distribution of Iraq's oil revenue directly to its people—Iraq has a good chance of beating the oil curse. To ensure that this happens, a provision should be incorporated into the new Iraqi constitution enshrining the right of each Iraqi household to receive a share of the country's oil proceeds. This right would extend for a minimum period of, say, ten years. The justification for this forfeiture of traditional Westphalian sovereignty is straightforward: it would prevent future Iraqi governments— even democratically elected ones—from changing the arrangement for the given period. After it expired, the people of Iraq could, through the democratic process, determine their own arrangements for managing future oil proceeds.

This temporary forfeiture of traditional sovereignty, frustrating though it may be, would actually uphold and strengthen the underlying sovereignty of the Iraqi people. It may be the only practical way to develop democratic institutions free of the corrupting influence of oil and to ensure the long-term economic and political empowerment of ordinary Iraqis.

The international community, ideally in the form of the UN, would supervise the implementation of this proposal. With some UN officials now under investigation for mishandling oil-for-food funds in the 1990s, more effective arrangements for transparency and accountability would have to be developed under the new system. Iraq today is an intrinsically more open environment than it was during the sanctions era. Greater involvement by civil society and the Iraqi people themselves—who would assert their constitutional right to claim their share of the oil resources— would help ward off mishandling and misappropriation of the funds.

The direct distribution of oil proceeds to the people could also help resolve the problem of Iraq's foreign debt. Many new democracies, such as Nigeria, have tried to get their external debts lifted, especially when a sizable part of the debt is "odious" (that is, contracted by previous dictators, often with the creditors' complicity). But donors will be justifiably wary of absolving the debts of a fledgling, faction-ridden Iraqi government. Transferring oil proceeds directly to the people rather than the government could allay this fear and hence make donors more amenable to granting debt relief.

Just how much of Iraq's oil revenues should be distributed? On the one hand, the more that goes to the population, the less the chance that oil will spoil the new Iraq. On the other hand, 100 percent distribution is probably infeasible. The new Iraqi government will face pressing needs, notably the rehabilitation of an infrastructure ravaged by the recent war and years of neglect under Saddam Hussein, as well as the servicing of some of its international debt. In the short run, financing these expenses through taxation will be unrealistic because Baghdad's machinery of taxation remains rudimentary. Some oil revenues should thus be retained by the government. But at least 50 percent should be distributed to the people.

In the long run, and not just in Iraq, the international community needs to put pressure on oil companies, which too often abet local corruption. For example, during the last several years, some thirty-four multinational oil companies paid the Angolan government to extract and refine its oil without ever disclosing where the money was going or what it was being used for within Angola. The international community should push governments and oil companies for greater transparency in the governance of natural resources. Collective action is key, however, since it is not in the interest of any one company to become transparent and honest on its own. Such collective action can be ensured through coordinated efforts by government, the private sector, and civil society. Many efforts have already been made in this regard, including the Extractive Industries Transparency Initiative sponsored by the United Kingdom's Department for International Development—although so far with limited success. Real efforts must also be made to crack down on corruption. Western countries should pass laws analogous to the EU's attempts to make the bribery of foreign officials a crime, and build on the UN's Convention against Corruption.

If the Iraqi experiment succeeds, the result will be a major boon—and not just for Iraqis. A success in Iraq would also provide a powerful example for other resource-rich countries to follow, illustrating how they could improve their economies and political systems. Resource-rich countries must realize that change, even radical change, is less risky than maintaining the status quo, in which oil continues to wreak the kind of damage it has so often around the world.

5

Iraq's Last Window:
Diffusing the Risks of a Petro-State

JOHNNY WEST

Headed for Normal—But What Kind of Normal?

Despite many wobbles, Iraq finally seems headed for some kind of normalcy in the years ahead. Political violence and insecurity remain tremendously high when compared to most other countries in the world, but are lower than the high point of 2007–08 and continuing to fall. The political process is riven with crises yet has survived five electoral processes and the best part of a year without an agreed government. Economic development is also in the wind, as oil revenues have crept up first on the back of the global commodities boom and then on Iraq's ambitious plans to expand its own production.

But to the question, what kind of normalcy, the answer so far is worryingly clear: a bloated petro-state that controls most of the economy, employs most of the workforce, and represents a mother-lode of patronage likely to provoke continuing rent seeking and competition, which in a society with Iraq's recent past is likely to take on sectarian and partisan undertones. The single biggest factor driving this trend is not any particular party or ideology, or the nature of certain domestic or regional actors and their complex interactions. It is the political economy of oil, as established in the growing body of evidence around the resource curse.[1] One bank account at the Federal Reserve Bank of New

First appearing in September 2011, this chapter has not been updated to reflect recent events.

York receives the proceeds of Iraq's oil exports from around the world and provides the vast majority of state income for this country of 32 million people.[2] All forms of taxation, meanwhile, hover collectively at 2 percent of government income. Clearly, to expect fully representative government in such a context would be optimistic at best. Influence, like the patronage that underlies it, is imbalanced and mostly one way. It should not, therefore, also be a surprise that nearly a quarter of Iraq's population lives below the national poverty line even though the country is classified as middle income.

But there is an alternative. In the immediate aftermath of the 2003 war, several eminent economists and development scholars suggested considering the concept of a significant oil dividend to be distributed directly to Iraqi citizens, in addition to revenues flowing into the state budget. In 2004 Nancy Birdsall and Arvind Subramanian proposed a ten-year guarantee to be written into the Iraq constitution, that a dividend of at least 50 percent of oil revenues be distributed to Iraqi citizens.[3] Steven Clemons proposed that a dividend from an investment fund be handled in the same manner as in the U.S. state of Alaska, while Thomas Palley argued for a dividend directly taken from oil revenues, without the intermediation of an investment fund.[4] These suggestions were not adopted, and in the intervening period a new state elite has established itself with spending and development patterns, as shall be seen below, that confirm the rationale of introducing the dividend in the first place.

Today, however, a new window of opportunity beckons. Under former Oil Minister Hussein Shahristani, Iraq finally managed to get contractual frameworks into place that will enable it to expand production considerably in the next few years. The oil is there and cheap to produce. While a host of political, regulatory, security, and infrastructural challenges remain, there is an expert consensus that Iraqi production—and revenues—will rise dramatically in the next few years. In this context it becomes possible to formulate a significant oil dividend that could dramatically alter Iraq's social and economic development for the better, transform its political culture, and cement all of its citizens' relationship with the Iraqi state—all while maintaining government spending plans at their 2011 levels.

What follows is an exposition of how such a fund could be calculated in the years leading up to 2015 using conservative assumptions about production, exports, and global markets; what the economic impact could be if the fund is harnessed to other development initiatives; how such a dividend could be implemented building on existing mechanisms in Iraq; the impact it could have on management of the oil industry itself and on various transparency processes currently in play; and, finally, how it could be viable politically. In fact, such a dividend program is already being actively considered by certain parts of Iraq's political spectrum.

Rise in Revenues Expected

As of early 2011 Iraq's production had still not topped the 2.4 million barrels a day it was producing at the time of the 2003 war—of which 1.9 million barrels were exported. But, as noted earlier, a series of far-reaching agreements were signed with international oil companies in 2009–10 to develop new and existing oil fields that promise to raise production dramatically. Hussein Shahristani, then oil minister, set Iraq's official production target at 11 to 12 million barrels of oil a day by 2016.

Industry predictions for Iraq's future production vary widely. While most experts would acknowledge that the proven reserves exist to justify the official target—unlike so many parts of the world, Iraq has nearly zero "geological risk"—a skeptical general view regards these numbers as generated only for public consumption.[5] This view maintains that the official figures are part of a narrative intended to justify the re-introduction of the international oil companies to Iraq almost four decades after nationalization, in the face of the intense economic nationalism. Expanding oil production to as much as 12 million barrels per day would be unparalleled in the history of the industry and would be hampered by continuing security, political, and infrastructural obstacles. Skeptics point out the fact that Iraq still has not even managed to reach pre-war production levels of crude. Nevertheless, the stage is set with the new service agreements, which are explicitly tied to achieving production plateaus field by field, and industry consensus certainly sees a rise in production in the coming years.[6] The question is by how much.

In late 2010 the World Bank based a $250 million development loan on projections showing production rising to 3.1 million barrels a day in 2012, a compound increase of almost 10 percent a year since 2010.[7] Assuming growth at the same rate through 2015, Iraq would by then be producing 4.3 million barrels a day, with exports rising to about 3.7 million barrels a day, an accumulated increase of 94 percent in the five

years from 2011 through the start of 2016.⁸ This could result in a considerably increased Iraqi take in the coming years and suggests that an
oil dividend is compatible with aggressive government plans for capital
public expenditure to get Iraq's economy and society back on track.
Exactly how much of an increase is subject, of course, to the vagaries of
market price. The International Monetary Fund (IMF) has published
conservative estimates of $68 per barrel in 2011 and $70.50 in 2012 for
Iraqi crudes and projects a rise in the government take by 30 percent
from just under $51 billion in 2010 to just over $66 billion in 2012.⁹
The IMF similarly projects from the same assumptions on price and production that budget deficits, which ballooned to nearly $15 billion in
2009, will be closed by the end of 2012.¹⁰ Assuming a constant price for
Iraqi crude of $70 per barrel through the end of 2015, together with
increased production at the rate projected above, Iraq would be earning
just short of $100 billion a year from its oil exports in five years time,
compared to $50 billion in 2010.

This gives ample scope for considering an oil dividend to citizens in
addition to public spending, as long as government spending is kept
around current levels. Both the World Bank and the IMF stress the need
for fiscal discipline in their continuing consultations with the government of Iraq, probably partly in response to the recent past.¹¹ When
crude markets soared to unprecedented heights in 2008, Iraq's oil take
leapt to over $60 billion, 60 percent higher than the year before. But
government spending soared even higher, leaping an astonishing 75 percent from 2007 to 2008. About a quarter of the increase was classified
as expanded public investment to rebuild the country's dilapidated
infrastructure. The remainder was a rise in current expenditures,
mostly salaries and pensions, and goods and services provided by the
government.

Leading officials in the government of Prime Minister Nouri al-
Maliki explained the spending decisions as a response to the long-term
trends of critical underinvestment and underpayment of public salaries
that Iraq had experienced as a result of war, isolation, and civil strife.
The budget shrank in 2009, but not by nearly as much as revenues fell
from plummeting world markets, and a substantial fiscal deficit opened.
In this sense, Iraq fell prey to one of the classic syndromes of oil-
producing countries: growing dependency on oil rents combined with

severe income volatility. Longer term, a new spending plateau of around $75 billion was established by the 2008 boom, which both the government and the international financial institutions (IFIs) envisage continuing at least through the end of 2012.[12]

This suggestion for a partial oil dividend is broadly in line with economic planning by the government of Iraq and the international financial institutions (IFIs). It assumes that public spending will rise moderately, at slightly over 2 percent a year, in line with Iraq's annual population growth over the past few years, allowing both the civil service and public investment to remain at current levels. It also conservatively assumes the government's non-oil revenues would rise at about one trillion dinars ($850 million) per year, below levels achieved in recent years and discounting the sizeable likely secondary effects of the dividend itself on government revenues.[13]

As the accompanying table shows, these constraints still allow a dividend beginning at $222 per adult Iraqi citizen in 2012, rising to $1,954 per adult in 2015, when the current parliament is due for re-election. From 2012 to 2016, total dividends of $73 billion would be distributed directly to the Iraqi population. This would be in addition to government spending as currently set by the 2011 budget.

This projection assumes no savings or contributions to a sovereign fund. The question of what proportion of funds might best be allocated to a savings or sovereign fund for countries in different stages of development is broadly debated. While many have cited the Norwegian model, others have concluded that this model cannot be appropriately exported from either a governance or a developmental perspective.[14] This chapter's projections for a dividend program are primarily illustrative given conservative assumptions about government spending, global markets, and Iraq's expansion plans. Clearly, however, by 2015 there should be considerable scope for both an oil dividend and contributions to a sovereign wealth or other fund,[15] and, it should be noted, as long as Iraq does not relapse into outright civil war, 2015 is likely to be closer to the profile of a typical financial year for the country going forward than 2011. Left out here is a more advanced and nuanced debate to tease out the detail of if and how such building of savings and financial portfolios should be begun, and how they would be dovetailed with the annual dividend to citizens.

TABLE 5-1. Projected Oil Price, Production, Revenue, and Dividend

	Oil			Budget ($ billions)		Dividend		
Year	Crude ($ per barrel)	Production (mbpd)	Export (mbpd)	Income	Spending	Population (million)	Deficit ($ billions)	Dividend (per capita)
2011	68	2.80	2.2	69.41	76.95	32.18	−7.54	
2012	70.5	3.20	2.6	81.44	77.8	32.88	3.64	222
2013	70	3.58	2.98	92.34	79.51	33.61	12.83	764
2014	70	4.01	3.41	104.18	81.26	34.35	22.92	1,335
2015	70	4.05	3.9	117.33	83.04	35.10	34.29	1,954

Sources: IMF, World Bank estimates to 2012; author calculations based on United Nations Population Fund and World Bank data to 2015.
Mbpd = millions of barrels per day

Economic Effects of a Dividend

In economic and development terms, such a dividend would have multiple effects. It could drive huge progress toward Iraqi fulfillment of the Millennium Development Goals (MDGs), eliminating income poverty in Iraq and helping to create conditions for pro-poor health services. It would represent continual stimulus for broad economic growth and diversification away from dependence on fossil fuels. Structured in the right way, it also has potential to drive small and medium enterprise (SME) growth, establish inclusive financial services, and power capitalization of the Iraqi economy from a broad domestic base that would take it in a new and unprecedented direction. On the downside, some economists raise concern that such a release of cash could create inflation. Each of these considerations is dealt with in detail below.

Iraq's Household Socio-Economic Survey (IHSES), completed in 2009, laid the foundation for poverty reduction in the country for the next decade.[16] Using a national poverty level of 76,896 Iraqi dinars (US$65) per person per month, IHSES established a clearly defined profile of poverty in Iraq as widespread but shallow.[17] Some 22 percent of the population was below that level. But at the same time the poverty gap was only 4.5 percent, meaning that it would require just over a billion dollars a year, distributed in the right way, to bring the entire population up above the poverty line. The poverty gap is, of course, a notional measure, and such a perfect distribution could not occur in the real world.[18] Nevertheless, the dividend as recommended here represents amounts that dwarf the poverty gap and would essentially eliminate poverty in Iraq.[19] Within two to three years, pockets of deep poverty, whether urban, such as in parts of Sadr City, or rural, such as in the villages of Muthanna, would indeed become history, and Iraq could move onto the next stage of economic development more typical of a middle-income country.

If the dividend alone ensures compliance with MDG 1 (the reduction of poverty), spending patterns among its beneficiaries might result in considerable inroads in MDGs 4 and 5 (relating to maternal and infant mortality).[20] In addition, MDG 3 targets universal primary education.

How Iraqis would choose to spend their dividends is, of course, unknowable. Nevertheless, a body of indirect evidence is accumulating to show that the kind of cash infusion the dividend brings could have strong positive impacts on all these indicators. For example, not only are large-scale, conditional cash transfer programs demonstrating positive impact more and more consistently,[21] in countries as diverse as Mexico, Malawi, and Brazil, but some evidence shows that the benefits may be more a result of the cash itself than the conditionality imposed by the schemes.[22]

As a kind of stimulus, the dividend is likely to represent a large incentive for the development of goods and services in the Iraqi economy compared to even the same amount of money allocated either to more government spending programs or financial sterilization programs. The natural ramping up provided by the gradual increase in oil rents over the next few years would give the embryonic private sector time to develop businesses against a fixed schedule to address a market of known size, an important incentive in a business environment as uncertain as Iraq's. It is thus not just the dividend's scale but its relative predictability that could catalyze poor-centric businesses in Iraq of the kind postulated by the late C. K. Prahalad in his book *Fortune at the Bottom of the Pyramid*.

Iraq's private sector has notched up a mixed record since the 2003 war. Sectors such as construction and the supply of commodities like wheat have often failed to serve the public well, while others such as telecoms have succeeded strongly.[23] But by creating massive new purchasing power that lies largely beyond the long arm of government patronage, as either monosponist or licensor and regulator, the dividend would be indisputably the biggest opportunity for private sector development the country has seen. Unsurprisingly given Iraq's circumstances, the public sector has represented over 80 percent of gross domestic product (GDP), and the IMF sees that proportion declining only slowly over time, projecting, for example, that the state will still account for over 75 percent of GDP in 2012.[24] If that projection held, mere distribution of the dividend would double the size of Iraq's private sector economy by 2015, even under the most unlikely conservative assumption—namely, that every single dinar of it would be consumed directly on foreign imports supplied by foreign companies with no Iraqi value added.

In fact, any private sector response to the opportunities of these new markets would likely address another of the chronic distortions caused by Iraq's oil wealth—an underdeveloped labor market. The World Bank states that Iraq has the lowest employment-to-population ratio in the Middle East region. Only 38 percent of working age adults are employed, with another 7 percent unemployed and the remaining 57 percent not in the labor market. Entrepreneurial initiatives to serve new consumption markets created by the dividend would likely create tens of thousands of private jobs, significantly expanding the sector.

However, the dividend would likely have another benefit: the reinvestment of significant sums into the economy from its newly capitalized population, either directly as sums put toward small businesses or as collateral for bank loans. Both the Iraqi government and international actors such as the World Bank and the U.S. Agency for International Development (USAID) have adopted microfinance as a key economic growth and diversification strategy, with the government creating a specialized ministry.[25] According to a USAID report in late 2010, nearly a quarter of a million loans have been made in the years since 2003, with $558 million disbursed. The aggregated portfolios of the twelve microfinance institutions (MFIs) that operate across the country stood at $100 million in 2010 with 70,000 clients.[26]

Clearly, the mere access of funds to poor Iraqis who fall into the target demographics for microfinance is far from sufficient, as successful microfinance and inclusive financial services, such as savings and insurance schemes, are complex ecosystems built on sound technical practice by the MFIs and networks that capture the human and social capital of the informal sector.[27] But equally clearly, the sheer size of funds available, and the fact that many of the addressable markets the dividend could create would be among Iraqis of limited income, could be transformative. If just 5 percent of the dividends were invested in SME and microfinance activities and the same number of jobs were created as USAID has posited for the microfinance sector to date,[28] the effect would be to create or sustain more than 1.3 million jobs in the SME sector, comfortably more than Iraq's current official unemployment rate. Benefits would be maximized to the extent that MFIs and their sponsors, both governmental and international, were able to integrate the dividends into their strategies in forms such as matching-loan products.

Further up the income scale, the dividend represents an opportunity to capitalize the economy from within. Iraq's economy is badly under-capitalized, even assessed in traditional terms and by conventional business practices, before any consideration of questions of social inclusivity. The World Bank reports that nearly two-thirds of the country's entire assets are held by two state-owned banks that date from the time of the former regime and are the only financial institutions to have nationwide branch networks.[29] The vast majority of these assets in turn belong to the state.[30]

Lending to the private sector amounted to just $3 billion in 2008, the year of Iraq's maximum windfall oil rents, and is mostly characterized by loan periods of less than twelve months. If the conventional banking system could capture 25 percent of Iraqi's dividends as savings in the years up to 2015, it would yield $18 billion, multiplying the private assets in the system many times over and most likely supplying the conditions for revival of the financial sector as a whole. As with microfinance, the extent of benefit extracted depends heavily on the degree to which existing players integrate the dividend into their strategies. But the dividend has the potential to be an extraordinary catalyst.

The previously discussed plans to reform Iraq's rationing and subsidies system also provide some strong synergies with the idea of a dividend. The World Bank has been in dialogue with the government of Iraq since 2005 on the possibility of reforming the Public Distribution System (PDS), instituted in the 1990s in response to sanctions. The system is still widely used by Iraqis, including many middle-class families, but represents a burden on government spending that reached $5.5 billion on this system in 2008, more than was spent on either health or education services.[31] The Bank is suggesting gradual reform, recognizing the iconic nature of the system and the service it provides, as well as the political infeasibility of abolishing it. The issue chiefly revolves around the inefficiency of the mechanism. The World Bank has estimated that more than $6 are spent for every $1's worth of goods delivered to the public. In addition, the PDS spawned the highest-level corruption case in recent years when former minister Abdel Fulah al-Sudani was indicted on charges of embezzlement in mid-2009. An oil dividend that would provide higher effective support to every household in the country even in its first year than does the PDS now would free the government and the Iraqi public to decide how best to proceed in reforming rationing and government-supplied commodity systems, knowing that a more efficient social safety net was already in place. Up to a tenth of the government's current budget could be reallocated to other social spending, boosting public health and education services, if the PDS inefficiencies were removed.

Objections to the concept of oil dividends have been based on perceived dangers of inflation and exchange-rate destabilization. But it should be noted that these are generic risks associated with the distribution of oil rents, known as Dutch disease,[32] and observed in dozens of natural resource–dependent economies around the world. The curbing of inflation is one of Iraq's rare successes in the past few years, and the impact a return of high inflation would bring, particularly on the disadvantaged, should not be dismissed lightly. At the same time, such risks attach to any policy that releases foreign currency flows inside the producing economy, including the government's current spending plans.

To the extent that a dividend would more effectively distribute revenues, it is true that it would represent some increased risk of inflation. Construction and real estate are a particularly vulnerable sector, already subject to Iraq's population boom, and care would need to be taken to avoid the distorting effects of one natural resource rent—oil—being replaced by another—land. Against that, an IMF working paper recently argued that a major cause of inflation in Iraq in recent years was the conflict itself.[33] Broadly speaking, levels of violence have been decreasing for three years now, and the impact of the dividend itself on political stability (explained below) could further significantly reduce the likelihood that it will contribute to inflation. Plus, coordinated integration of the dividend into economic development at all levels, as outlined above, would sharply reduce inflationary pressure. Finally, the graduated nature of the dividend, rising with Iraq's increase in production, allows absorptive systems to grow and strengthen in response to real market conditions.

Impact on Oversight of the Oil Industry

As described, the dividend proposal would go in hand with current government spending levels and alongside existing mechanisms to manage
oil rents. As such it could strongly bolster efforts to oversee Iraq's oil
industry as it grows and the revenues it generates. This is becoming a
more complex sector by the month, as the international oil companies
and their secondary contractors set up operations in the country.

As noted above, since the 2003 war all the revenues from Iraq's
export sales have flowed into one account at the Federal Reserve Bank
of New York, where it is monitored by a United Nations–appointed
committee called the International Advisory and Monitoring Board for
Iraq (IAMB).[34] Iraqi state-owned enterprises have been solely responsible for exporting and selling the country's oil during that time. Iraq has
been in the position of having one bank account for export revenue
whose records are published on the Internet, "a level of transparency
unparalleled for oil dependent countries in the region," according to the
World Bank.[35] As a UN-mandated mechanism, the account has been
immune to any claims on Iraq for debt or reparations apart from a
5 percent set-aside decreed by the UN to go toward compensation to
Kuwait for the 1990 invasion.

But the arrangement Iraq maintains with the Federal Reserve, which
has been extended every year since 2006, is due to change in 2011.
There has been increasing pressure for the government of Iraq to implement replacement arrangements that will likewise guarantee due dili-
gence in monitoring Iraq's oil revenues. As of early 2011 discussions
were ongoing.

It would be misleading to say that even under the present arrangements all of the money flowing from Iraq's oil has been accurately
accounted for. The Development Fund for Iraq (DFI) account in New
York represents simply one point along the long chain of revenue flows.
It pays most of its money to the Ministry of Finance, which then allocates funds to other government ministries as part of the budget process.
Most, but not all.

Downstream from the DFI, transfers of billions of dollars go directly
to other ministries and state-owned entities. Because of the lack of clar-
ity as to how these parallel accounts are disbursed, they must effectively
be considered off-budget, and, indeed, the World Bank has set a goal of

helping the government to establish a single treasury account to conform with best practice when possible. Meanwhile, the IMF has been working with the Central Bank of Iraq to trace ownership and provenance of some 9.8 trillion dinars ($8.3 billion) in the banking system. As of June 2010, 2.1 trillion dinars in ministry accounts remained unaccounted for, while another 4.6 trillion dinars remained unaccounted for in accounts held by other state entities, such as pension funds and state-owned enterprises including the oil companies. That makes a total of 6.7 trillion dinars ($5.7 billion) of assets in the banking system of uncertain provenance, something over 20 percent of total assets. Opacity within Iraq's financial system is such that the IMF reported in October 2010, for example, that the Central Bank of Iraq "has started" to report international reserves it holds. The Open Budget Index gave Iraq a score of absolute zero for the transparency of its 2010 budget and budget process, at the bottom of ninety-four countries surveyed.[36]

Iraq faces even larger transparency challenges upstream of the DFI account. Theft of crude oil and refined products has run to billions of dollars a year since 2003, through bunkering, false-bottomed tankers and ships, and pipeline siphoning.[37] At times major pieces of infrastructure such as the Baiji refinery and even parts of Basra port and terminal appear to have come under the control of armed groups linked to the insurgency. Forcible seizure and attacks are decreasing, however, as security improves, and smuggling of crude, as opposed to refined products, seems to have been successfully checked by former Oil Minister Hussein Shahristani's gradual lifting of state subsidies. Nevertheless, systemic checks remain lacking. Seven years after the Coalition Provisional Authority commissioned the U.S. firm KBR to introduce metering to measure the amount of oil flowing from the well-heads and through the system for refining and export, the latest attempt at metering is still well behind schedule.[38]

In addition, the new involvement of the international oil companies (IOCs) has created whole new upstream areas of contracting, licensing, and expense reporting, which require new monitoring systems still not in place. Although some features of the fifteen agreements, signed with IOCs such as BP, Shell, ExxonMobil, Eni, Total, Gazprom, and China's CNPC, are public, many more are not, including "cost recovery," the terms under which the companies will be able to claim tens of billions of dollars of capital investment in new infrastructure to deliver the increases in production.[39] In addition, the primary contractors, IOC-led consortia, have already begun subcontracting to service companies in potentially multimillion-dollar deals without scrutiny.[40] As operations ramp up on the ground, the IOCs' relationships with branches of the Iraqi state are extending from the Oil Ministry to other ministries in Baghdad, various security forces, two levels of local government, border and immigration authorities, and state-owned enterprises, some of which are run at arm's length from accountable state control. Any of these interactions represents potential points of leakage in accountability.

The good news is that, as well as the DFI account, the Iraqi government has moved to increase accountability through the Extractive Industries Transparency Initiative (EITI), announcing its candidacy in early 2010. EITI is an international policy instrument, established in 2002, under which governments and oil companies both declare their payments to a neutral third party auditor, appointed by a board made up of representatives from both sides—plus, critically, civil society groups to ensure its independence. As of early 2011, some thirty-five countries were at various stages of implementation. Iraq's entry is significant as the first major Middle Eastern producer, and officials are confident they can meet requirements for full validation by early 2012. Iraq has already been publishing information required for its first report on aggregated export quantities and sales.

But EITI is purposely an instrument of limited scope. The global-level board and management describe their role as aimed at building trust and creating space for wider debates about natural resource transparency.[41] Like the DFI mechanism, it is a snapshot of one point in the value chain. Moreover, for its second report, Iraq will have to expand information included to cover at least the primary contracts with the IOCs. Debate continues over the degree of granularity in the numbers to be published.[42]

The picture of accountability of the oil industry in Iraq is, therefore, promising in parts. And yet a complex ecosystem that is only partially transparent is not fundamentally transparent at all, since the "bubble effect" simply allows leakage and mismanagement to migrate from a well-monitored part of the system to a lesser one. Even a partial misuse of oil funds has broad overall impact on Iraq's political life, society, and standard of living by leading to rent seeking, nepotism, and communalism in public office. The total cost of a ten million dollar embezzlement is many times that, if, in order for that to happen, the wrong people have sought office for the wrong reasons and, quite apart from issues of personal integrity, are unable to formulate policy and manage.

There has been much emphasis in recent years on technical mechanisms such as fiscal stabilization funds, sovereign wealth funds, and ring-fenced mechanisms to direct oil rents toward designated social spending. None of these has yet been introduced in Iraq although the World Bank and IMF have referred to government consideration of a formal stabilization fund.[43] But as far as accountability goes, the accumulated global evidence suggests that any such mechanism is only as good as its surrounding governance environment. The crowning proof of this is perhaps the ill-fated Chad-Cameroon pipeline, supported for many years by the World Bank, which anticipated that the project would demonstrate how natural resource projects could enhance social development. In the end the Chad government undermined carefully negotiated agreements and spent oil money on weapons once the $4.5 billion export pipeline had been built with World Bank credit guarantees.

A dividend program, in and of itself, does not address issues of oversight directly. But it transforms the stakeholder landscape. The reason such a program has potential to improve governance is not *what* it does to monitor revenues, but *who* it brings to the table. While a broad and ongoing debate about the effectiveness of initiatives such as EITI and various technocratic-led initiatives to create better governance around oil and natural resources ensues, two things are clear about the status quo.[44] First, overall, these initiatives have met with limited success globally as supported by a sizeable body of evidence about the link between natural resource–dependent economies and slower economic growth, civil war, and other forms of strife.[45] Second, such initiatives are limited to small numbers of actors, whether "insiders" such as host country or international experts and civil servants, or "outsiders" such as national and transnational civil society groups. The EITI process in Iraq has not reached the public or media, beyond event-driven official announcements. A United Nations Development Program survey in late 2010 showed no awareness of the EITI process objectives and mechanisms, either among educated segments of the population or the media.[46]

It is difficult to avoid the conclusion that the second element (limited size of the actors engaged in transparency initiatives) of the picture is related to the first (limited success of such initiatives, not the dividend). But a dividend delivered annually to 15 million Iraqi adults, with a "scorecard" for the remainder of the oil rents that stay in government hands, can make management of the oil industry a matter of intense public interest. It would be an event on the political calendar, as it is in the U.S. state of Alaska, the only large jurisdiction currently operating an oil dividend program.[47]

Moreover, public scrutiny would be influenced by the very real shared interest to keep the industry going. There would be an incentive, in other words, to build consensus around policies and management that was optimal rather than perfectionist. This is noteworthy in the Iraqi context since the current government's approach to management of the industry does not go unchallenged. Some Iraqi politicians maintain that all contracts with IOCs should be approved by the Iraqi parliament, as was the case under the previous regime and other political dispensations in the region influenced by Arab nationalism, such as Egypt and Syria. The government counters by saying the nature of the contracts allows management by executive decree—by the Iraqi cabinet, in other words.[48] But the industry is now being developed in the absence of a comprehensive legal framework. Although clear regulation of the industry was one of the four milestones set by the George W. Bush administration, four draft laws governing various aspects of the industry have been hung up in parliament since 2007 and show no sign of being resolved.

A dividend program cannot eliminate all the various policy debates in Iraq about how the industry should be run. But it can reframe the discussion, in light of the strong self-interest of every adult Iraqi citizen to see those issues resolved. There would be as much pressure on oppositionists to be responsible as on government officials to be accountable. The politics of oil could begin to be reshaped as aggregations of pragmatic self-interest, with the public engaged through competing platforms, rather than held by large-scale public ignorance, cynicism, and apathy, and, at best, some kind of confessionally based rotation of oil rents through patronage networks running through all levels of the government. The oil industry, in other words, could begin to be led by policy rather than partisanship.

Political Considerations

A universal oil dividend, based on Iraqi citizenship, could reorder—and strengthen—the relationship between the Iraqi citizen and the state and consolidate the state's territorial integrity. Although one of the objections sometimes raised with regard to the dividend concept is that it weakens the state, this equates the strength or weakness of the state simply with the amount of money it accumulates. Perhaps more crucial than revenue flows is the actual legitimacy of the state, especially in postconflict environments such as Iraq. A dividend cannot by itself override all other considerations in a citizen's relationship with the state. Yet it could invert the top-down and unaccountable tradition of government that still pervades Iraq and forge a new relationship in which the state—and its legitimately elected governments—begins to live up to claims of serving the Iraqi people.

Specifically, a dividend could have a critical and positive impact on Iraq's Kurdish issue. Since 1991 the north of Iraq has been under the control of Kurdish *peshmerga*, armed militants, from the two historic parties that formed the Kurdistan Regional Government (KRG).[49] The regional government in Erbil and the central government in Baghdad have a complex relationship characterized by bitter disputes in a number of areas and working accommodations in others.[50] This precarious balance has only been maintained by KRG leaders who value regional autonomy and have largely stopped short of any move toward outright independence.[51] But the autonomy of the three provinces of Iraq officially designated as the KRG over the last two decades is now wide and deep, and most of the five million people in this area have little direct contact with the Iraqi state.

In this context the universal dividend acts as a strong soft power to retain Iraq's territorial integrity. If every Kurd in Iraq were the recipient of a substantial dividend each year because of Iraqi citizenship, the other long list of disputes—management of the oil industry, the right to export directly, the extent of the territories that should fall under KRG control—would all take place within an overarching framework of the Iraqi state. Although there has been no substantial Kurdish-Arab fighting since 2003, political analysts agree that the Kurdish dispute could trigger conflict even more destabilizing than the Sunni-Shia struggles of 2005–08.[52]

It is worth bearing in mind that although the KRG has developed its own contractual framework for the oil industry, signing deals with up to forty IOCs, over two-thirds of oil production comes from Iraq's southern provinces around Basra, an output likely to be maintained through the coming expansion of the industry. Thus, a countrywide dividend could yield as much to each Kurdish citizen as a regionwide measure, especially if the Kurds maintain control over the three provinces of Erbil, Suleimaniya, and Dohuk.

The idea of some form of regional entity has also come and gone among certain political currents of the South in recent years. The Islamic Supreme Council of Iraq touted this idea until it was trounced across the south in provincial elections in 2009, but it has not gone away and is likely to re-emerge.[53] Perhaps in response to this attempt at greater regional autonomy, the government introduced what it called the "petrodollar" in the 2010 budget. This allocates directly one dollar for every barrel of oil produced to provincial administrations, with a compensating formula for non–oil producing provinces (NO). By late 2010 Iraqi media were full of reports of plans and contracts toward which provincial governments such as Kirkuk and Basra were putting their "petrodollars."

While the need to recognize local communities is important in management of natural resources, the petrodollar approach risks creating perpetual debate over its fairness. Is the level of one dollar enough? Are the formulas designed for the non-producing provinces fair? It is an unfortunate fact in the history of oil that while production in many areas has caused severe disruption to local communities, attempts to redress local interests, which are based on the sense that producer regions are more entitled to the oil and its revenues, can be destabilizing. This is one factor that links oil production with secessionist movements, such as those in Kabinda in Angola, in the Niger Delta in Nigeria, or in West Papua.

The oil dividend makes it easier to differentiate between who owns oil—in this case all Iraqis—and who is most adversely affected by its development. Careful plans for developing a field, and the accompanying projects to create local employment and protect the environment, are necessary in order to compensate those who live close to the producing areas, not because they own the oil more than other Iraqi citizens, but because they are most affected by its development.

Similarly, the sense of shared ownership changes the dynamic of insurgent activities designed to hamper production, although it has sometimes been hard to distinguish whether attacks against oil facilities are politically motivated sabotage or organized crime.[54] Between 2003 and 2008 there was an average of two attacks a week on the industry and its employees, and even though security has improved, attacks continue. In part because of these attacks, Iraq exported only 1.9 million barrels of oil per day in 2010—200,000 barrels per day short of its target. To try to counter the problem, the head of Iraq's specialized oil police, Major General Hamid Abdullah Ibrahim, remarked in early 2011 that he had 30,000 men under his command and that Prime Minister Nouri al-Maliki had agreed to add another 12,000.[55] However, a dividend would create a different dynamic for any armed groups with political ambition, because their constituencies in Iraq, like all others, would be direct beneficiaries. Attacks leaving your potential supporters much worse off would be harder to justify.

More generally, beyond the extremes of secessionist movements and violent insurgencies, the dividend would decrease the proportion of Iraq's rent that could be accessed through the offices of the Iraqi state—and therefore decrease the incentive for rent seeking within the government. Together with implementation of other parallel development measures discussed above, a dividend program could contribute to depoliticizing Iraq's government and civil service.

Another option for the Iraqi government—one that could transform the political culture—is to use the dividend to extend the country's tax base. Taxes averaged a fraction over 2 percent of revenues in the years 2007–10 and are expected to rise only gently to 2.4 percent by 2012.[56] Exact figures are not easily available, but it is clear that entire sectors of the population—and the economy—work outside the tax system. The dividend would be a rare opportunity to encourage citizens to register for potential taxation, even if the option of actual taxation were deferred or introduced gradually.[57] In this way, the country could begin to move toward the basis of real representative politics and away from one of the key factors of the resource curse, the dissociation of the political elite from the electorate.

Mechanics of a Dividend

Legally, the Iraqi parliament would pass a bill approving a direct dividend, either as an absolute amount or as a percentage of revenues earned over a particular period, and specify the modalities of defining those revenues.

Technology has made distributing small payments to a large number of recipients vastly easier, as attested by the rise of cash transfer initiatives across the developing world in recent years.[58] Large-scale systems in Mexico and Brazil now register administrative costs of under 5 percent. A system could be developed in Iraq combining mobile phone access to accounts bolted onto as much pre-existing infrastructure, such as banks and microfinance institutions, as is feasible and efficient. Given the pace of implementation of a nationwide geometric ID system in India, a similar project could likely be completed in Iraq within two years at low cost if security considerations could be overcome.[59]

The experience of M-Pesa in Kenya also demonstrates that a cell-phone-based cash transfer system can be quickly established.[60] Nearly 20,000 distributors of mobile phone credit in Kenya, a country broadly comparable in size to Iraq, have already signed up as M-Pesa agents to administer cash payments, and the potential base is 100,000 distributors in small shops all over the country.

Iraq has promising pre-conditions for implementing a similar scheme. A competitive mobile phone market is one of the country's great post-2003 successes with nearly 20 million subscriptions across five competing national networks.[61] Networks such as Zain and AsiaCell already provide extensive value-added information services and have departments devoted to expanding their products. In addition, the Public Distribution System (PDS) offers a nationwide identification infrastructure that has already been used for the electoral roll in Iraq's 2004 and 2009 elections. The World Bank estimates that 99 percent of Iraqi families own a PDS ration card.[62]

Iraq remains underbanked with only 550 branches for its twenty-nine banks across the entire country—clearly insufficient to service every potential dividend holder who may have an account in one of these bank branches. Nevertheless, if the PDS infrastructure, the banking system, MFIs, and the phone networks can be leveraged, the logistical challenge of establishing an annual payment system in Iraq seems perfectly manageable and also compatible with security concerns, since most of the money in the system at any one time would be in accounts or electronic form of some kind rather than cash.

The Political Moment?

The Arab Spring and the entry of the populist Sadrist movement into Nouri al-Maliki's second governmentmay make the most promising moment to consider a dividend policy since Iraqis took over the political process from the Coalition Provisional Authority in 2004. In the March 2010 elections both the Sadrists and some members of the Fadhila Party advocated some permutations of it.[63] In October 2010 the Sadrists joined Maliki's coalition, bringing forty deputies into parliament to support his bloc, and were allocated seven ministers in the government. Cabinet sources said the Sadrists suggested a 15 percent allocation of oil revenues to dividends during budget negotiations, but the proposal did not make it into the final budget, submitted to parliament at the end of February 2011.

Nevertheless, that fiscal 2011 budget approved by Maliki and his senior ministers showed that they realized that the Iraqi public was beginning to lose patience over the failure of successive governments to deliver basic public services, despite the tens of billions of dollars flowing into the coffers. Another petrodollar fund was established, of one dollar for every barrel produced, to be allocated directly to local authorities around the country according to need and population weight. Plans to spend nearly a billion dollars on F-15 fighters were shelved, and the savings were allocated to increasing food rations.

The stage seems to be set for a dividend. Oil revenues were a major issue in popular protests all across the country in February and March 2011, during which dozens of people were killed and the governor of oil-rich Basra was forced to resign. One protest banner in Baghdad's Tahrir Square read, "The oil of the people is for the people, not for the thieves."[64]

The Sadrists, with strong support among the Shia poor, still advocate a dividend, and could perhaps influence other political entities, such as Maliki's Islamic Dawa Party, which is at least in partial competition for the same constituency. The attitude of other actors, such as parties with a support base among Sunni Arabs, is less certain.

Before the protests, an editorial by Jaber Habib Jaber, a former pro-fessor at Baghdad University and current ambassador to the United States, in the respected pan-Arab newspaper *al-Sharq al-Awsat* on January 16, 2011, captured the new mood, citing the continuing economic hardship and post–Arab Spring turmoil in the Middle East and the call by Muqtada al Sadr himself for direct distribution of revenues.

> We cannot ignore the difficulties of the idea of distributing part of the oil revenues to every individual in a country where a proper census is lacking. But this is the last call to confront this problem before it becomes too entrenched, and to seek a way for oil to avoid becoming the reason for repeating the tragedies of the past.

Despite the push to consider a dividend, mainstream thinking within Iraq's government ministries and established parties is likely to remain skeptical of the value and feasibility of even a partial dividend. While no particular party stands out as chief opposition, the political class as a whole seems to fear that a dividend could disrupt the status quo.

Conclusion

This chapter advocates a dividend that is universal and unconditional. It is precisely these features that create a paradigm establishing the rights of the populace to a publicly owned good—the country's natural resources—as enshrined in the Iraqi constitution. A dividend program would engage strong support across a social spectrum and does not necessitate a complicated state mechanism, with its attendant bureaucracy, to identify and administer to a particular target group.[65]

Because a dividend program already is emerging as part of Iraq's political discourse, wide and open debate soon of the options is crucial. Such a debate as to whether an oil dividend is suitable, and, if so, in what form, could build consensus across different parts of the country's fractured political spectrum. This would surely be better than to leave the issue to one faction or party and subject to the norm of partisanship both in support and in application.

After the fall of the regime following the 2003 war, several leading scholars advocated an oil dividend program before a new state elite had a chance to entrench itself. That did not happen, and while in the intervening period the reconstruction process has made some headway in Iraq—it could hardly do otherwise—improvements have fallen short of most citizens' expectations. Something over $300 billion has already been earned in oil revenues since 2003 and gone into the public purse but without what most Iraqis would see as commensurate returns.

The expansion of the industry expected in the next few years, with the increased revenues it will bring, represents another golden opportunity. It would be feasible politically, economically, and socially for the government to issue its first universal oil dividend of around $220 per adult on October 3, 2012. Indeed, the opportunity may not come around again for many years.

Notes

1. Jeffrey Sachs and Andrew Warner examined the resource history of ninety-seven countries over a period of eighteen years, 1971 to 1989, and found that states with a high abundance of natural resource exports had abnormally slow economic growth in general, relative to other countries. See Sachs and Warner, "Natural Resource Abundance and Economic Growth," Working Paper 5389 (Cambridge, Mass.: National Bureau of Economic Research, 1995). Others have challenged the idea of the resource curse more recently, most notably Christa Brunnschweiler and Erwin Bulte in "The Resource Curse Revisited and Revised: A Tale of Paradoxes and Red Herrings," *Journal of Environmental Economics and Management* 55, no. 3 (2008), pp. 248–64, and Halvor Mehlum, Karl Moene, and Ragnar Torvik, in "Cursed by Resources or Institutions?" *World Economy Journal* 29, no. 8 (2006), pp. 1117–31.

2. Oil accounts for over 80 percent of government revenues.

3. "Saving Iraq from Its oil," *Foreign Affairs* 83, no. 4 (2004) pp. 77–89.

4. See Steven Clemons, *Sharing, Alaska Style* (Washington, D.C.: New America Foundation, April 9, 2003) (www.newamerica.net/publications/articles/2003/sharing_alaska_style), and Thomas Palley, *Combating the Natural Resource Curse with Citizen Revenue Distribution Funds: Oil and the Case of Iraq* (FPIF Special Report, December 2003), hosted on the website of the Open Society Institute.

5. In October 2010 Iraq raised its estimate of proven reserves by 24 percent to 143 billion barrels, placing the country second behind Saudi Arabia in terms of conventional crude oil reserves. Officials and international experts concur that reserves figures are likely to rise even higher as exploration, part of the service agreements signed with international companies, continues using technologies new to Iraq.

6. The consortium led by ExxonMobil, for example, which won the bid for the service agreement in the West Qurna Phase One contract area, is contractually committed to raising production levels from 244,000 barrels a day in late 2009 to 2.1 million barrels a day and holding it there for seven years. British Petroleum, operating in the Rumaila field, has guaranteed to take production there from just over a million barrels a day to 2.85 million barrels a day by the end of the next decade.

7. World Bank, *First Programmatic Fiscal Sustainability Development Loan*, Report 51528 (Washington, D.C., February 2010), p. 5.

8. Annual growth of 10 percent might be a reasonable estimate for aggressive expansion, brokering between the zero geological risk and contractual frameworks on the one hand and the multitude of logistical and security issues on the other. The 3.7 million figure assumes domestic demand for oil rising slightly as development and spending power increase, bearing in mind that Iraq has phased out fuel subsidies. In addition, some energy demand, such as for electricity, may then be met by gas production, which Iraq is now undertaking for the first time.

9. Iraq exports two crudes, the Basrah and Kirkuk grades. Both have historically traded at slight discounts to the Brent benchmark, but another important factor in the size of oil rents is that costs of production in Iraq are estimated to be among the lowest in the world. In 2010 a conservative estimate of market price saved Iraq from a far worse fiscal deficit than it actually had. Exports then fell short by almost 10 percent of expectations, but the aggregate price per barrel turned out to be $72 on world markets against the government estimate of $63.50.

10. International Monetary Fund, "Iraq: First Reviewer under the Stand-by Arrangement," Country Report 10/316, October 2010, p. 15.

11. "Staff urged the authorities to use conservative assumptions for oil exports and prices in preparing the 2011 budget . . . while making every effort to contain current spending." See ibid., section 13.

12. Iraqi government figures for 2010–11 and IMF predictions for 2012. See ibid.

13. The IMF projects non-oil revenues rising from 13.2 trillion dinars ($11 billion) in 2007 to 17.8 trillion dinars ($15 billion) in 2012. These figures include revenues earned by state enterprises in the oil and energy sectors as well as other funds from the industry, such as signature bonuses, but excludes oil export revenues. See ibid.

14. Norway's Government Pension Fund was estimated in 2010 to own assets worth $350–400 billion, representing about $80,000 for every Norwegian citizen. Notably, Paul Collier argues in *The Plundered Planet* (Oxford University Press, 2010) that developing countries both need and can absorb higher proportions of natural resource rents as capital investment compared to Norway, which developed its oil industry when it was already economically developed.

15. Broad political and governance conditions under which such funds can flourish should also be taken into account, a discussion touched on in the section on management of the oil industry below.

16. Conducted in consultation with the World Bank, field surveys collected information from some 18,000 households and 127,000 individuals across the country in 2006–07.

17. At about $780 a year in real currency terms (using an exchange rate of 1,183 Iraqi dinars to the dollar), this national poverty level is considerably higher than the UN-set definition of poverty at $730 per year using the Parity Purchasing Power (PPP) method of calculating GDP (the ratio in figures for real versus PPP-GDP figures, according to the World Bank, is 1.37).

18. The poverty gap represents an imaginary figure needed for a perfectly targeted distribution that would bring an entire population up to the poverty line. Those with income above the level are discounted, and the sum needed to bring up those who fall below the line is aggregated, then expressed as a percentage of the amount of money generated by the total population earning that level of income.

19. The multiple starts at 3 in 2012, rising to 10 in 2013, 18 in 2014, and 27 in 2015. From 2013 the dividend itself equals the income needed for an individual to escape poverty.

20. MDG 4 targets a reduction in child mortality by two-thirds in percentage terms between 1990 and 2015, while MDG 5 aims for reduction in maternal mortality by three-quarters over the same period.

21. The Oportunidades initiative in Mexico and Bolsa Família in Brazil are gaining increasing attention from development economists.

22. David Hulme, Joseph Hanlon, and Armando Barrientos, *Just Give Money to the Poor, the Development Revolution from the Global South* (Sterling, Va.: Kumarian Press, 2010), p. 56.

23. World Bank, *Considering the Future of the Iraqi Public Distribution System* (Washington, D.C., June 28, 2005).

24. IMF, "Iraq: First Reviewer under the Stand-by Arrangement," p. 13.

25. Microfinance programs include USAID's Tijara and the World Bank's Fiscal Sustainability program, as well as the SME components in USAID's Tatweer program and UNDP's Private Sector Development initiative.

26. See www.iraq-businessnews.com/2010/11/09/usaid-tijara-plans-microfinance-conference/.

27. Specifically, microfinance programs as evolved classically by Mohammed Yunus at Grameen Bank require guarantees from a peer group, a principle similar to informal co-operative lending societies in many developing countries.

28. The USAID Tijara statement that $558 million has created or sustained 203,000 jobs to date gives a ratio of $2,748 per job. That ratio applied to 5 percent of the dividend by 2015, or $3.68 billion, would represent 1,340,399 private jobs.

29. The World Bank's *First Programmatic Fiscal Sustainability Development Loan* states that banks account for more than 90 percent of assets and that the Rafidain and Rasheed banks hold more than 70 percent of these assets.

30. The World Bank's Report 51528 (ibid.) estimates overall assets at $26 billion, while the IMF estimates government assets held in commercial banks, including Rafidain and Rashid, to total 29 trillion dinars, or about $24.5 billion (see IMF, "Iraq: First Reviewer under the Stand-by Arrangement").

31. See World Bank, *First Programmatic Fiscal Sustainability Development Loan*, Report 51528.

32. The term *Dutch disease* comes from the effects first perceived in the Netherlands after the influx of high revenues from natural gas fields discovered in the North Sea in the 1950s. But it is important to note that the Netherlands did not give out dividends and any effects were created by expanded government spending and other macroeconomic programs.

33. David Grigorian and Udo Kock, *Inflation and Conflict in Iraq: The Economics of Shortages Revisited,* Working Paper 10/159 (Washington, D.C.: IMF, 2010).

34. The IAMB was established as part of the Development Fund for Iraq by UN Security Council Resolution 1483 in May 2003.

35. World Bank, *First Programmatic Fiscal Sustainability Development Loan*, p. 15.

36. See www.internationalbudget.org/files/2010_Full_Report-English.pdf.

37. Phil Williams, *Criminals, Militias and Insurgents: Organized Crime in Iraq*

(Carlisle, Pa.: U.S. Strategic Studies Institute, 2009) (www.strategicstudiesinstitute.army.mil/pdffiles/pub930.pdf).

38. PricewaterhouseCoopers reported in its September 2010 audit report to IAMB that while 3,300 meters were supposed to be in place, as part of an overall plan to install 4,900 meters, only 1,690 had been installed. A large proportion of these had also not been calibrated to the specifics of the grades of crude that flow through them, leaving a margin of error larger than industry norms, while at least six different types of meter had been procured, which is likely to make effective system maintenance difficult for the foreseeable future.

39. Televised auctions were held for the agreements in which consortia bid on two published variables: the fee accepted as a service remuneration per barrel of oil produced and a production plateau guaranteed for a given number of years. But the agreements contain many other clauses dealing with financial, social, and environmental aspects, which were negotiated privately. Model agreements published reveal the general outline of the contract structures but little to none of the negotiated detail.

40. For example, a $224 million deal was announced in 2010 by state-owned Missan Oil Company to work with Weatherford in Missan province.

41. Oxford economist Paul Collier, asked to consult in 2008 on EITI's future, described the initiative as "the right place to start and absolutely the wrong place to stop" in natural resource governance.

42. EITI allows both disaggregated and aggregated reporting. At one end of the spectrum, complete aggregation such as in Azerbaijan would be just one specific figure of so many billion dollars for the total of exchanges between the government and all natural resource companies. At the other end, disaggregation as in Liberia involves publication of payments broken down company by company and into types—tax by tax, duties, excise, signature fees, and so on.

43. World Bank, *First Programmatic Fiscal Sustainability Development Loan*, Report 51528.

44. Among international institutions engaged in supplying technical advice on management of the industry are the IMF, via ROSC (Reports on the Observance of Standards and Codes) evaluations; the World Bank's Oil, Gas and Mining Group; the Bureau for Development Policy with UNDP; Norway's Oil for Development program; and various regional development banks.

45. Sachs and Warner in "Natural Resource Abundance and Economic Growth" and Collier in *The Plundered Planet*.

46. UNDP, "Assessment of Iraq's EITI," internal document (New York: United Nations, 2010).

47. In Alaska the dividend was originally announced every September by the state revenue commissioner, a civil servant. In recent years, however, it has become a fixture of the governor's office.

48. After several years of debate, Iraq's Supreme Court in 2010 upheld the government's interpretation by rejecting litigation brought by former parliamentary deputy Shata Musawi against the government and the oil company British Petroleum on these grounds.

49. The two parties were the Kurdistan Democratic Party founded by Mustafa Barzani and the Patriotic Union of Kurdistan led by Jalal Talabani, now federal president of Iraq.

50. In terms of the oil industry, Kurdish leaders dispute Baghdad's definition of which oil fields are "producing," as defined in the 2005 constitution. They claim the right to set up and manage their own contracts with oil companies and have signed deals with some thirty companies, which Baghdad does not recognize. At the same time, each year a percentage of the budget will be transferred to KRG, and in early 2011 there were reports that the two sides had privately reached agreement to fix the KRG region's contribution to Iraq's export levels for 2011 to 100,000 barrels per day.

51. The speech that Masoud Barzani, president of the KDP, gave at the party's conference in December 2010, in which he said self-determination would be the party's guiding principle, including possible independence, was controversial precisely because he challenged the convention established in recent years

52. The International Crisis Group, in its report on Arab-Kurdish clashes in the province of Ninewa in 2009, stated: "The bloodshed and institutional paralysis are symptoms of the country's shifting battle lines: from an essentially Sunni versus Shiite sectarian struggle, mainly centred in the capital, to a predominantly Arab against Kurdish ethnic fight playing out along an extended axis of friction." See International Crisis Group, *Iraq's New Battlefront:The Struggle over Ninewa*, Middle East Report 90, September 2009.

53. International Crisis Group, *Iraq's Uncertain Future: Elections and Beyond*, Middle East Report 94, February 2010, p. 14.

54. Phil Williams, in *Criminals, Militias and Insurgents: Organized Crime in Iraq*, demonstrates that an attack on the Kirkuk-Ceyhan pipeline represents an opportunity for oil theft through the tanker fleet that has to be used as a substitute. There also seem to have been complex interactions where gangs may have paid local armed insurgents a cut to acquiesce in or facilitate the theft.

55. See *Iraq Oil Report*, January 28, 2011 (www.iraqoilreport.com/security/energy-sector/no-country-for-oil-smugglers-5301/).

56. IMF, "Iraq: First Reviewer under the Stand-by Arrangement."

57. Paul Segal, *Resource Rents, Redistribution, and Halving Global Poverty: The Resource Dividend* (Oxford, UK: Oxford Institute for Energy Studies, 2009).

58. Todd Moss, *Oil to Cash: Fighting the Resource Curse through Cash Transfers*, Working Paper 237 (Washington, D.C.: Center for Global Development, January 2011).

59. Infosys CEO Nandan Nilekani first proposed the idea of giving 700 million Indians over the age of eighteen unique geometric identification cards early in 2009. It is on schedule to be completed by the end of 2011 at a cost of about $5 per head, according to Nilekani (www.hindustantimes.com/Each-Unique-ID-number-costs-Rs-100-Nilekani/Article1-633800.aspx).

60. M-Pesa began in March 2007. By the middle of 2010, according to *The Economist*, it had gathered some 9.5 million subscribers, was responsible for transfers equal to 11 percent of Kenya's GDP, and had inspired some sixty other schemes around the world including in environments as tricky as Afghanistan.

61. The International Telecommunications Union 2010 statistical abstract states that there were sixty-four subscriptions for every 100 people in Iraq in 2009 and that mobile phone ownership had doubled every year since 2004 (www.itu.int/ITU-D/ict eye/Reporting/ShowReportFrame.aspx?ReportName=/WTI/CellularSubscribersPublic

&ReportFormat=HTML4.0&RP_intYear=2009&RP_intLanguageID=1&RP_bitLive Data=False).

62. World Bank, *First Programmatic Fiscal Sustainability Development Loan.*

63. Sheikh Sabah al-Sadi, head of the Iraqi parliament's anticorruption committee, told the author in conversation that he had advocated that 25 percent of oil revenues be placed in a savings account for each Iraqi citizen.

64. See www.iraqoilreport.com/politics/national-politics/analysis-protests-alter-political-landscape-5419/.

65. Paul Segal cites evidence to show that social programs that are targeted tend to become less well resourced over time because they suffer from a lack of political consensus. See Segal, *Resource Rents, Redistribution, and Halving Global Poverty.*

Contributors

Nancy Birdsall is president of the Center for Global Development (CGD).

Scott Goldsmith is professor of economics, University of Alaska–Anchorage.

Jay Hammond was the former governor of Alaska 1974–82.

Todd Moss is vice president and senior fellow at CGD.

Arvind Subramanian is senior fellow at CGD and the Peterson Institute for International Economics.

Johnny West is a journalist and founder of Open Oil.

Index

The Center for Global Development

The Center for Global Development works to reduce global poverty and inequality through rigorous research and active engagement with the policy community to make the world a more prosperous, just, and safe place for us all. The policies and practices of the rich and the powerful—in rich nations, as well as in the emerging powers, international institutions, and global corporations—have significant impacts on the world's poor people. We aim to improve these policies and practices through research and policy engagement to expand opportunities, reduce inequalities, and improve lives everywhere. By pairing research with action, CGD goes beyond contributing to knowledge about development. We conceive of and advocate for practical policy innovations in areas such as trade, aid, health, education, climate change, labor mobility, private investment, access to finance, and global governance to foster shared prosperity in an increasingly interdependent world.